HOW TO BEST REGULATE CRYPTO-ASSETS?

The EU and UAE Perspectives

European Union Law Series

This series brings together major works in the field of European Union Law. It features a diverse range of publications, including comprehensive handbooks designed to teach European Union Law, treaties for legal practitioners and academics, monographs on specialised topics and some of the best doctoral dissertations from across Europe. Additionally, it includes publications detailing conference proceedings on topical issues, as well as commentaries on major judgments and decisions handed down by the Court of Justice of the European Union.

P. Durand and A. Gilbert-d'Halluin (eds.), *Directive (EU) 2022/2464 as regards Corporate Sustainability Reporting (CSRD)*, 2024.

G. Marti (ed.), *European Citizenship through the Lens of EU Values*, 2025.

A. Gridel, *Financial Markets and Instruments in Private International Law*, 2025.

G. Cavalier, *European R&D Tax Incentives. Contribution to the Emergence of a Concept*, 2025.

HOW TO BEST REGULATE CRYPTO-ASSETS?

The EU and UAE Perspectives

Pauline Pailler (ed.)

Preface by Dominique Legeais

Introductory Remarks by Philippe Richard

INTERSENTIA
LEFEBVRE GROUP

Intersentia
Lefebvre Belgium SA
Avenue Jean Monnet, 4
1348 Louvain-la-Neuve
Belgium
Email: contact@larcier-intersentia.com

Distribution for the UK, Ireland and
Rest of the World (excl. France, Belgium and Luxembourg)
Ingram Publisher Services UK
1 Deltic Avenue, Rooksley
Milton Keynes MK13 8LD
United Kingdom
Tel: +44 1752 202 301 | Fax: +44 1752 202 331
Email: ipsuk.customercare@ingramcontent.com

Distribution for France and Other Countries (excl. Ireland and the UK)
Interforum Editis
92 avenue de France
75013 Paris
France

Distribution for Belgium and Luxembourg (excl. France, Ireland and the UK)
Larcier-Intersentia
Avenue Jean Monnet, 4
1348 Louvain-la-Neuve
Belgium

ISBN : 978-1-83970-581-6
D/2025/06040/0710
NUR 820

British Library Cataloguing in Publication Data. A catalogue record for this book is available from the British Library

LIST OF AUTHORS

André Abou Aad
Lawyer

Maria Luisa Babo Rodrigues
Enforcement and Regulatory Affairs Manager for VARA

Ruben Bombardi
Head of Regulatory Enablement and General Counsel for VARA

Thierry Bonneau
Professor of Law, Paris-Panthéon-Assas University

Hubert de Vauplane
Partner, Morgan Lewis

Pablo Guédon
Associate Professor in Private Law, Clermont-Auvergne University, Michel de l'Hospital Research Center

Jack Hardman
Partner, Clifford Chance

Dominique Legeais
Professor of Law, Paris Cité University

Matthias Lehmann
Professor, University of Vienna and Radboud University Nijmegen

Ryan Lemand
Founder and CEO of Neovision Wealth Management

Nicholas McNicholas
Head of Regulatory Affairs and Enforcement for VARA

Diego Montes Serralde
Regulatory Enablement and Legal Manager for VARA

Edmond O'Hanlon
Legal Counsel, Financial Services Regulatory Authority

Pauline Pailler
Professor of Law, Paris Cité University – Director of CEDAG – Member of the Institut Universitaire de France

Philippe Richard
Executive Director, International Affairs, FSRA

Clément Saudo
Director of the financial market and crypto-assets services division, Legal Affairs Department, AMF France

FOREWORD

Pauline PAILLER

How to regulate crypto-assets is a fundamental political and economic issue. In this regard, the United States provides a highly symbolic example: following a significant policy shift under President Donald Trump, the country enacted the GENIUS Act *(Guiding and Establishing National Innovation for U.S. Stablecoins)* on 18 July 2025. This legislation marked a clear pivot towards a more supportive regulatory framework for crypto infrastructure, especially stablecoins. The regulation of crypto-assets affects competitiveness, market attractiveness, and, crucially, sovereignty – particularly monetary sovereignty in the case of stablecoins or central bank digital currencies. While the United States has long treated crypto-assets as equivalent to other regulated instruments, in particular securities, other jurisdictions such as the United Arab Emirates (UAE) and the European Union (EU) have, from an early stage, striven to provide regulatory clarity and predictability for those operating in the crypto sphere, as well as to offer frameworks specifically tailored for crypto-assets. Comparing these different models is particularly insightful: although the core regulatory challenges are broadly similar, the diversity of approaches highlights the range of possible policy responses to the evolving digital asset landscape.

The method of adopting the rules in the two regions under consideration is specific and complex. In the United Arab Emirates, this complexity is heightened by the need to balance the interests of the individual emirates, some of which are international financial centres – in particular Abu Dhabi and Dubai – with those of the federal government. Thus, the regulatory architecture involves various authorities.[1] These include the Financial Services Regulatory Authority (FSRA) of the Abu Dhabi Global Market (ADGM),[2] the Dubai Financial Services Authority (DFSA) of the Dubai International Financial Centre (DIFC), the Virtual Assets Regulatory Authority (VARA),[3] the Central Bank of the UAE, etc.

1 R. LEMAND, 'The UAE: A Magnet for Global Finance'; A. ABOU AAD, 'Regulation of Professionals in the Emirates'.

2 E. O'HANLON, 'Taxonomy of Digital Assets in the Emirates: The FSRA Model'.

3 M.L. BABO RODRIGUES, D. MONTES SERRALDE, N. MCNICHOLAS, and R. BOMBARDI, 'Comparative Analysis of the EU MiCAR and the VARA Regulatory Regime for Virtual Assets'.

In the European Union, the interests of the 27 Member States must also be considered, which raise issues of competitiveness. However, particular attention should be given to the standard-setting process in the EU, which is unique in its structure. The regulatory framework involves several levels. First, Level 1 texts include primary legislation (regulations or directives) adopted by the European Commission, the Council of the European Union, and the European Parliament. In the field of crypto-asset regulation, the cornerstone text is the MiCA Regulation.[4] Secondly, Level 2 texts consist of delegated and implementing acts adopted by the European Commission based on the Level 1 framework.[5] These provide the detailed rules necessary to implement, in practice, the principles established in the Level 1 texts. Finally, Level 3 texts include non-binding instruments such as guidelines, opinions, and statements developed by the European Supervisory Authorities, namely the European Banking Authority (EBA) and the European Securities and Markets Authority (ESMA).[6] This multi-layered system of rule-making significantly contributes to the overall complexity of the regulatory framework for crypto-assets.

Each of the key themes related to crypto-assets – including central bank digital currencies,[7] crypto-asset taxonomy,[8] stablecoins,[9] supervision of crypto-asset service providers,[10]applicable law,[11] and tax regime[12] – is examined, to present a comprehensive overview of the regulatory landscape in both the UAE and the EU.

This book is the result of the publication of the proceedings of the symposium held on 20 February 2025 at Sorbonne University Abu Dhabi. It would not have been possible without the valuable contributions of all the speakers, to whom I would like to express my sincere and heartfelt thanks[13].

---

4 Regulation (EU) 2023/1114 of 31 May 2023 on crypto-asset markets (MiCA Regulation).

5 As of 21 July 2025, there were 25 delegated regulations and 7 implementing regulations from the European Commission. See https://www.esma.europa.eu/sites/default/files/2025-07/ESMA75-113276571-1510_MiCA_Level_2_and_3_table.pdf.

6 Ibid.

7 See J. Hardman, 'CBDCs in Emerging Markets and the UAE's Digital Dirham Example'; T. Bonneau, 'The Digital Euro Package of June 2023'.

8 E. O'Hanlon, 'Taxonomy of Digital Assets in the Emirates: The FSRA Model'; P. Pailler, 'The MiCA Regulation Methodology: Strengths and Limits'.

9 H. de Vauplane, 'Stablecoin Regulation in MiCA'; E. O'Hanlon, 'FSRA Stablecoin Regulation'.

10 C. Saudo, 'Crypto-asset Service Providers in MiCA'; M.L. Babo Rodrigues, D. Montes Serralde, N. McNicholas, and R. Bombardi, 'Comparative Analysis of the EU MiCAR and the VARA Regulatory Regime for Virtual Assets'; A. Abou Aad, 'Regulation of Professionals in the Emirates'; P. Pailler, 'AML and Crypto-assets: The European Regulatory Framework'.

11 M. Lehmann, 'Choice of Law under MiCAR: Applicable Law and Competent Court for Crypto-assets, Services and Offers'.

12 P. Guédon, 'The European Tax Regulation of Crypto-assets'.

13 I would like to express my sincere gratitude to Charlotte Rieger for her careful review of the contributions of this volume.

PREFACE

Dominique Legeais

The title of this symposium acknowledges a twofold development. On the one hand, there is no longer any doubt that crypto-assets are well established and are reshaping the face of finance. There are new products, new players, and new operations. Monetary, banking, and financial law must adapt accordingly. On the other hand, regulation has become essential. This second assertion was less obvious. If we recall the initial ambition, it was to establish a world of freedom based on the libertarian model, in opposition to the fiat world, which symbolised constraints. In fact, in the early years, the crypto economy developed around the world without constraints. But this return to the 'Wild West' and this new quest to make an easy fortune very quickly revealed certain features that were unacceptable to many states. There was, firstly, a threat to existing legal currencies. However, this attack on monetary sovereignty has been repelled by the majority of states. Various scandals and scams, such as that involving FTX, have also discredited the system. Regulation has, therefore, gained ground and has even been called for by major players in the crypto economy.

This is because regulation has clear merits. It provides legal certainty and, therefore, confidence for stakeholders. It establishes fundamental rules for any market: transparency, investor protection, the imposition of constraints on service providers, and compliance with anti-money laundering and terrorist financing measures. Even the most liberal countries have finally acknowledged the benefits offered by regulation.

However, while becoming increasingly widespread, regulation has also become a major factor in competitiveness. Each country must attract this new finance and its new players. The US example clearly illustrates this. Regulation can be more or less liberal, both in terms of the applicable legislation and the practices of the regulatory authorities.

This conference, therefore, makes perfect sense, comparing regulation in the UAE and in the EU, which are in fact two pioneering models. The choice to examine the conditions for better regulation is particularly relevant. The UAE has been very quick to embrace the crypto economy, as well as emerging technologies such as AI. It rapidly put in place an attractive regulatory system to support this policy. This is a major focus of its development. The MiCA Regulation was the first to establish comprehensive regulation of crypto-assets. In both cases, there is a central bank cryptocurrency project.

However, these two legal systems are exploring different paths. The comparison shows greater pragmatism and liberalism on the part of the UAE. Its choice of English law is not neutral; it is more adaptable and pragmatic. The regulation put in place is intended to be resolutely attractive, and is accompanied by a particularly attractive tax regime. The MiCA Regulation had the same ambition. It was supposed to be a model for all legal systems. However, the limitations of the MiCA Regulation have been quickly brought to the fore. It appears to be very complex to implement. The list of Level 1, 2, and 3 texts is illustrative. At the same time, it seems incapable of answering all the questions that have arisen since its implementation. Finally, it is not always easy to determine which rules will apply to the range of innovative products that are constantly being developed. Questions of classification are becoming essential. The taxonomy of crypto-assets is, therefore, essential.

These weaknesses in the MiCA Regulation are all the more apparent when compared with US law, which is now the benchmark, raising new issues. With the passing of the GENIUS Act and various other pieces of legislation, the United States now wants to be seen as a leader in the crypto economy. Dollar-based stablecoins should benefit from this favourable legislative environment. Other legal systems must now adapt to this new situation. It would, indeed, be paradoxical if an innovation intended to undermine traditional finance ultimately resulted in strengthening the dominance of the dollar. Other systems must, therefore, react very quickly to remain attractive.

The work of the symposium thus makes it possible to consider alternative solutions and compare their respective merits. More fundamentally, this work contributes to the reflection taking place in all countries on how to put in place sufficiently stringent regulation to preserve certain imperatives while allowing a degree of freedom to maintain interest in crypto-assets and attract players in the crypto economy.

TABLE OF CONTENTS

PART 2
UAE'S DIGITAL DIRHAM VERSUS EU'S DIGITAL EURO PACKAGE

PART 3
WHAT MODEL FOR REGULATING CRYPTO-ASSETS?

Title 1
TAXONOMY OF CRYPTO-ASSETS

Title 2
THE REGULATION OF STABLECOINS

Title 5
TAX REGIME

INTRODUCTORY REMARKS

Philippe Richard

Let me start by saying a few words about the Financial Services Regulatory Authority (FSRA) and Abu Dhabi Global Market (ADGM): FSRA is the internationally recognised risk-based regulator of Abu Dhabi Global Market, aligned with best practices and international standards (IOSCO, BCBS, IAIS, etc). In that context, we carefully monitor what is going on in the EU, particularly with MiCA. At the same time, we are a progressive regulator supportive of financial innovations. We are technology-neutral and mostly demand-driven, protecting investors and contributing to financial stability, and, at the same time, facilitating market development. The question we ask when facing a financial innovation is always the same: should we forbid it, ignore it, or regulate it? For virtual assets (VAs), we identified their potential early and concluded that we should regulate these new instruments. Ignoring or forbidding them would not work, in part due to their digital design and cross-border nature. However, we decided to regulate them progressively and in a pragmatic manner, creating a regime that balances innovation with strong regulatory oversight.

Technological innovation is transforming the financial services industry. Constant advances in new technologies have provided opportunities for significant change and disruption to financial services and other related activities globally. Developments in distributed ledger technologies (DLT) have led to the emergence of various types of digital assets, including stablecoins, digital securities, utility tokens and virtual assets for the facilitation of economic transactions or the transfer of value.

As you may know, ADGM and its regulator, FSRA, started the crypto – or, I should say, the virtual asset – journey several years ago, back in 2018. In our approach, we took several steps.

The first step was to define what we are talking about. This is surprisingly important when you realise that, even within the crypto industry, basic terms such as staking, decentralised finance (DeFi), or even stablecoin can have profoundly different meanings. The taxonomy discussion is extremely important in establishing a common language that allows us to have meaningful conversations about risks and opportunities. You will have a full analysis on this question with a comparison of EU/UAE and ADGM-specific context in the contribution of my colleague, Edmond O'Hanlon.[1] We came up with a broad definition of digital assets and a narrow definition of virtual assets.

The second step consisted in identifying the players and their activities. In 2020, the FSRA, with the benefit of a greater understanding of the scope of VA-related activities in ADGM, replaced the previous regulated activity of OCAB (that is, Operating a Crypto Asset Business) with amended descriptions of the following regulated activities, which could be undertaken in relation to VAs, namely:

- Dealing in investments as principal or agent, commonly referred to as broker/ dealer;
- Advising or arranging on investments or credit;
- Managing assets;
- Providing or arranging custody; and
- Operating a Multilateral Trading Facility (MTF), commonly referred to in the industry simply as a crypto exchange.

We also issued guidance setting out the FSRA's approach to the regulation of the use of VAs in ADGM. This guidance, together with the applicable ADGM Regulations and FSRA Rules governing the use of VAs, are collectively referred to as the 'Virtual Asset Framework'.

Consistent with the definition used by the Financial Action Task Force (FATF), the FSRA has defined VAs as follows: 'Virtual Asset; means a digital representation of value that can be digitally traded and functions as (1) a medium of exchange; and/or (2) a unit of account; and/or (3) a store of value, but does not have legal tender status in any jurisdiction.'

In the VA ecosystem, users can create, store, and transfer VAs without the need for any third- party intermediaries, like banks for fiat currencies. This creates a set of unique challenges for regulators worldwide. Without regulated entities controlling the creation and use of VAs, the system is open to misuse, for example in financial crime and other unlawful activities, at scale potentially including the contagion risks impacting on the stability of the financial sector. Also, unlike traditional markets with established global practices, there is no current safety net that ensures that users and investors will be able to recover their VAs, for example in case of loss or theft. Accordingly, the FSRA has addressed issues around consumer protection, safe custody, technology governance, disclosure/transparency, market abuse, and the regulation of Multilateral Trading Facilities using VAs, in a manner similar to the regulatory approach taken in relation to securities/derivatives exchanges globally.

---

1 See, *infra*, E. O'Hanlon, 'Taxonomy of Digital Assets in the Emirates: The FSRA Model'.

Let me mention another challenge we have had to face. Firms engaging in crypto-asset activities were required to meet specific prudential and conduct requirements, which included the use of only 'accepted' VAs with which such firms could serve clients. Accepted VAs (AVAs) required prior FSRA approval, granted upon the satisfaction of certain qualifying criteria, which focused on risks inherent to the specific VA as well as risks related to specific firms. This two-stage approach meant that a VA could be approved for use by some VA firms while not by others, depending on the adequacy of the systems and controls of the relevant VA firm.

When the FSRA assumed responsibility for the assessment of each VA in 2018, its decision was based on the potentially significant risks associated with a nascent VA sector and the relatively small universe of VAs in existence, of which only a limited number could meet the FSRA's traceability requirements. Today, the FSRA has approved 93 AVAs that firms in ADGM can offer to their clients.

The FSRA notes that the VA sector and the global regulatory landscape in respect of VAs have developed rapidly since the creation of the AVA approval process, and VA firms have gained experience operating in a regulated environment. Therefore, the FSRA now considers it appropriate to permit VA firms to play a more significant role in the assessment of VAs. For this purpose, the FSRA has proposed replacing the current FSRA-led AVA approval model with a self-assessment and notification process.

More recently, the FSRA introduced a regulatory framework for the issuance of stablecoins, or fiat-referenced tokens (FRTs), as we call them in ADGM, expanding the suite of digital assets that can be offered in a regulated environment. The formalisation of this framework follows extensive industry engagement and feedback received on a 2024 Consultation Paper.

The FRT framework introduces several key components that establish robust standards for FRT issuers to ensure financial stability and investor protection. For example, a specific rule on reserve assets will minimise the risks of variability in the value of FRTs by setting strict requirements on the constituents of reserve assets. Equally, from an innovation perspective, the FRT framework does not prohibit issuers from passing on a share of the earnings or yield of reserve investments to FRT holders, so long as the ability to maintain the par value is not compromised.

This balanced approach, benchmarked against international standards and best practices, positions ADGM at the forefront of financial innovation. This year, you can expect to see even more updates as we introduce amendments to our digital assets framework, for example in response to emerging business models such as staking of VAs, and VA borrowing and lending. As technologies advance, the need for adaptive regulations and collaboration between regulators and industry grows. At ADGM, we are not just excited by the opportunities;

we are actively working to create an ecosystem where new business models can flourish in safe markets, customer experiences are enhanced while being protected, and financial inclusion is meaningfully increased.

La Sorbonne AD, 20 February 2025

PART 1.

The Institutional Regulatory Framework

THE UAE: A MAGNET FOR GLOBAL FINANCE

Dr Ryan LEMAND*

SECTION I. INTRODUCTION

1. The United Arab Emirates (UAE) has rapidly emerged as a leading global hub for financial services, attracting substantial international investment and talent. This chapter examines the factors contributing to the UAE's attractiveness as a financial jurisdiction, with a particular focus on the pivotal role of international financial centres (IFCs), the unique legal and regulatory frameworks of its various jurisdictions, and significant recent developments such as the introduction of fund passporting.

SECTION II. THE STRATEGIC IMPORTANCE OF INTERNATIONAL FINANCIAL CENTRES

§ 1. DEFINITION AND KEY CHARACTERISTICS

2. An international financial centre is a strategically located geographic area that serves as a central hub for a wide range of global financial activities. An IFC provides the essential infrastructure and a robust legal and regulatory framework necessary to facilitate banking, trading, investments, and diverse financial services. Several key characteristics define a successful IFC:

1) Global Connectivity: IFCs possess strategic locations and are deeply integrated into the global financial network, enabling seamless transactions and interactions. This connectivity is often facilitated by a combination of factors, including geographical location, strong transportation links, and advanced communication technologies. For instance, London's location at the centre of the world's time zones, combined with its extensive network of flights and high-speed internet infrastructure, has been crucial to its success as an IFC.[1]

---

* ryan.lemand@neovision-wealth.com

1 G.L. CLARK, *Pension Fund Capitalism*, Oxford, Oxford University Press, 2000.

2) Robust Infrastructure: This encompasses a comprehensive ecosystem with advanced trading platforms, efficient clearing houses, and sophisticated foreign exchange services. A robust infrastructure is vital for the smooth functioning of financial markets. For example, the New York Stock Exchange (NYSE) relies on cutting-edge technology to handle massive trading volumes, while clearing houses like the Depository Trust & Clearing Corporation (DTCC) ensure the efficient settlement of transactions.[2]
3) Legal and Regulatory Framework: A critical attribute is an internationally recognised rule of law and a mutually recognised regulator with a rule book that adheres to the highest international standards, ensuring stability and investor confidence. A strong legal and regulatory framework is paramount. The predictability and enforceability of contracts under English common law, for example, have made London a preferred location for international financial transactions.[3]
4) Human Capital: The ability to attract and retain high-calibre talent is essential for an IFC's success, fostering innovation and expertise. IFCs are magnets for skilled professionals. Cities like Singapore and Zurich have invested heavily in education and training to develop a deep pool of talent in finance, law, and technology.[4]
5) Economic Impact: IFCs contribute significantly to both the domestic and global economies, driving growth and development through financial activities. The economic impact of IFCs is substantial. They generate employment, attract foreign direct investment, and facilitate the flow of capital across borders, contributing to overall economic growth.[5]

§ 2. FACTORS CONTRIBUTING TO AN IFC'S SUCCESS

3. A successful IFC is a dynamic location where 'capital, innovation, and opportunity meet', guided by an often 'invisible' conductor ensuring harmonious operation. This highlights the critical importance of a well-functioning ecosystem where diverse stakeholders can interact efficiently, fostering growth and stability. This involves not only a sound regulatory environment but also a culture of innovation and a supportive business climate.

---

2 J. Tilly, *Competition and Regulation in the Airline Industry*, Aldershot, Ashgate Publishing, 2006.

3 P.S. Davies, *Introduction to Company Law*, Oxford, Oxford University Press, 2010.

4 B.S.A. Yeoh, *International Migration*, London, Routledge, 2018.

5 S. Grassman, *The International Economy*, Harlow, Pearson Education, 2005.

§ 3. THE UAE AND THE GULF COOPERATION COUNCIL (GCC) AMIDST ECONOMIC AND GEOPOLITICAL SHIFTS

4. The UAE and the broader Gulf Cooperation Council (GCC) region are currently navigating a period of significant economic and geopolitical change. These shifts, which include global events such as those in the Far East (China/Taiwan) and Eastern Europe (Ukraine/Russia), are creating uncertainty in the global landscape. The UAE, however, is increasingly viewed as a safe and neutral haven, attracting substantial capital inflows through strategic infrastructure investments and offering robust intellectual property protection. The country also plays a vital role in capital export, further solidifying its financial influence. This safe-haven status is enhanced by the UAE's political stability, diversified economy, and strategic location.[6]

§ 4. IMPORTANCE OF INVESTMENT FUNDS FOR AN IFC

5. Investment funds are indispensable to the success of an IFC, offering a wide array of crucial benefits that enhance its attractiveness and functionality:

- Investment-level Impact:
  - Capital Attraction: Funds draw diverse global investors, significantly boosting both local and international financial influence.
  - Asset Diversification: They support resilience by diversifying assets, appealing to a wide range of investor profiles and mitigating risks.
  - Innovation: Funds drive growth in emerging sectors such as fintech and green energy, fostering innovation and progress.
  - Job Creation: They fuel employment in finance, compliance, and advisory roles, contributing to economic growth.
- Legal Importance:
  - Investor Protection: A robust legal framework is essential to safeguard the interests of foreign investors, promoting confidence and trust.
  - Dispute Resolution: Efficient mechanisms for dispute resolution reduce risk and attract greater international capital flows.
  - Global Standards: Compliance with international laws and norms enhances the IFC's credibility and trustworthiness on the global stage.
- Regulatory Importance:
  - Market Stability: Effective regulatory oversight ensures transparency and protects against market volatility, maintaining a stable financial environment.

---

6 IMF, *United Arab Emirates: Staff Report for the 2023 Article IV Consultation*, International Monetary Fund, 2023.

- o Anti-Money Laundering (AML) and Know Your Customer (KYC) Compliance: Robust controls and procedures enhance the IFC's reputation as a secure and compliant centre for financial activities.
- o Investor Confidence: Transparency and accountability in regulatory practices attract institutional investors, who prioritise security and sound governance.

§ 5. REGULATORY CHALLENGES AND OPPORTUNITIES FOR IFCS

6. IFCs face several complex regulatory challenges, as well as promising opportunities, in the constantly evolving global financial landscape:

- Global Standards and Uniformity: The increasing push for more uniform regulations, particularly in critical areas like transparency, anti-money laundering, and tax compliance (for example, the OECD's Base Erosion and Profit Shifting (BEPS) initiatives), is significantly reshaping how IFCs operate. Adapting to these evolving standards is not merely a challenge but a necessity for gaining and maintaining global trust and credibility. The BEPS project, for example, has led to significant changes in how IFCs approach corporate taxation, requiring them to demonstrate substance and transparency to avoid being labelled as tax havens.[7]
- Compliance Emphasis: In the contemporary financial world, compliance is paramount. IFCs that excel in adhering to stringent Financial Action Task Force (FATF) guidelines, and which consistently maintain a whitelist status, are highly preferred destinations for family offices and institutional investors. These entities prioritise security, transparency, and regulatory compliance in an increasingly complex and interconnected financial landscape. The FATF's recommendations set the global standard for AML and counter-terrorist financing measures, and adherence to these standards is crucial for an IFC's reputation and competitiveness.[8]
- Opportunity in Emerging Markets: The rising economic influence of, and increasing interest from, rapidly growing regions like Asia, the Middle East and North Africa (MENA), and Africa present significant growth opportunities for agile and responsive IFCs. These centres must adapt to the specific needs and characteristics of these markets to effectively capture and capitalise on emerging opportunities. For instance, IFCs in the Middle East

[7] OECD, 'Base Erosion and Profit Shifting', 2024, retrieved from https://www.oecd.org/tax/beps/.

[8] FATF (ongoing), 'Financial Action Task Force', retrieved from https://www.fatf-gafi.org/.

are strategically positioned to facilitate investment flows between Asia and Africa, leveraging their geographical location and cultural ties.[9]

SECTION III. THE UAE AS A HUB FOR INTERNATIONAL FINANCIAL CENTRES

7. The UAE has strategically positioned itself as a leading global financial hub, boasting a sophisticated and dynamic ecosystem of IFCs. This section will explore the key financial centres within the UAE, highlighting their unique characteristics, contributions to the nation's financial landscape, and growing importance in the international arena.

§ 1. OVERVIEW OF THE UAE'S FINANCIAL REGULATORY FRAMEWORK

8. The UAE has established a robust financial regulatory framework comprising multiple authorities, each playing a distinct and crucial role in overseeing various financial sectors. This well-structured framework supports a dynamic and rapidly growing financial sector, ensuring stability, promoting investor protection, and fostering innovation across the financial spectrum. Key regulators within the UAE include the Securities and Commodities Authority (SCA), Abu Dhabi Global Market (ADGM), Dubai International Financial Centre (DIFC), the Central Bank of the UAE, and the Insurance Authority (now integrated with the Central Bank). This multi-layered approach allows for specialised regulation tailored to the specific needs of different financial activities, while also promoting overall coherence and stability within the UAE's financial system.[10]

§ 2. SECURITIES AND COMMODITIES AUTHORITY (SCA)

9. The Securities and Commodities Authority is the primary regulator of securities markets in the UAE. Its broad responsibilities encompass:

- supervising and regulating stock exchanges, such as the Abu Dhabi Securities Exchange (ADX) and the Dubai Financial Market (DFM), ensuring fair and efficient market operations;

---

9 World Bank, *Middle East and North Africa Economic Update, October 2023: Coping with Inflation and Debt*, World Bank, 2023.

10 UAE Central Bank (ongoing), 'Central Bank of the UAE', retrieved from https://www.centralbank.ae/en/.

- overseeing brokerage firms and investment funds, maintaining the integrity of these crucial financial intermediaries;
- enforcing corporate governance and disclosure requirements, promoting transparency and accountability among listed companies; and
- licensing and ensuring the ongoing compliance of financial institutions, upholding high standards of conduct and stability within the financial sector.

10. The SCA plays a vital role in maintaining investor confidence and market integrity, which are essential for attracting both domestic and international capital.[11]

§ 3. ABU DHABI GLOBAL MARKET (ADGM)

11. ADGM is a leading international financial centre located in the UAE capital. It operates with its own independent regulatory framework, distinct from that of the wider UAE, providing a unique and attractive environment for international financial activity. Key components of ADGM include:

- Financial Services Regulatory Authority (FSRA): The independent regulator responsible for authorising, supervising, and enforcing financial services activities within ADGM, ensuring adherence to the highest international standards. The FSRA's rule book is closely aligned with international best practices, fostering a regulatory environment that is both robust and conducive to business.[12]
- ADGM Courts: An independent court system based on English common law, providing a familiar, trusted, and efficient legal environment for international businesses and financial institutions. The ADGM courts are staffed by experienced judges from common law jurisdictions, ensuring a high level of judicial expertise and efficiency.[13]
- Regulatory Oversight: ADGM provides a comprehensive and sophisticated regulatory regime for a wide range of financial activities, including banking, asset management, fintech, and digital assets, fostering innovation and growth in these key sectors. ADGM has been proactive in developing regulations for emerging areas like fintech and sustainable finance, positioning itself at the forefront of innovation in the region.[14]

12. ADGM's adoption of English common law is a significant differentiator, making it the only jurisdiction in the Middle East that has adopted this

---

[11] SCA (ongoing), 'Securities and Commodities Authority', retrieved from https://www.sca.gov.ae/en/.

[12] ADGM FSRA (ongoing), 'Financial Services Regulatory Authority', retrieved from https://www.fsra.gov.ae/.

[13] ADGM Courts (ongoing), 'ADGM Courts', retrieved from https://www.adgmcourts.com/.

[14] ADGM (ongoing), 'Abu Dhabi Global Market', retrieved from https://www.adgm.com/.

highly respected legal system. This provides a high degree of legal certainty and predictability, which is particularly attractive to international financial institutions seeking a stable and reliable base for their operations. The choice of English common law was a strategic one, aimed at attracting international businesses familiar with this system and providing them with a legal framework they understand and trust.[15]

§ 4. DUBAI INTERNATIONAL FINANCIAL CENTRE (DIFC)

13. DIFC is another major global financial hub within the UAE, playing a crucial role in the region's financial landscape. It is governed by:

- Dubai Financial Services Authority (DFSA): The independent regulator of financial services conducted in or from DIFC, ensuring adherence to international best practices and standards. The DFSA is known for its rigorous and risk-based approach to regulation, which has contributed to the stability and integrity of the DIFC.[16]
- DIFC Courts: An independent court system, also operating within a common law framework, providing a robust and efficient mechanism for dispute resolution. The DIFC Courts have established a strong reputation for their efficiency and impartiality, providing businesses with confidence in the resolution of commercial disputes.[17]

14. DIFC's regulatory framework covers a broad spectrum of financial activities, including banking, insurance, asset management, and fintech. It also offers a tax-efficient environment for business, further enhancing its attractiveness to international businesses. The combination of a common law legal system, a strong regulatory framework, and a favourable tax regime has made DIFC a magnet for international financial institutions seeking a base in the Middle East.[18]

§ 5. VIRTUAL ASSETS REGULATORY AUTHORITY (VARA)

15. Dubai has established the Virtual Assets Regulatory Authority as a dedicated and specialised regulator for the rapidly evolving field of virtual assets. VARA is responsible for:

15 Al Tamimi & Company. 'ADGM: A New Era for Financial Services in the UAE', 2016, retrieved from https://www.tamimi.com/en/knowledge/publications/adgm-a-new-era-for-financial-services-in-the-uae.

16 DFSA (ongoing), 'Dubai Financial Services Authority', retrieved from https://www.dfsa.ae/.

17 DIFC Courts (ongoing), 'DIFC Courts', retrieved from https://www.difccourts.ae/.

18 Oxford Business Group, *The Report: Dubai 2023*, Oxford Business Group, 2023.

- licensing and regulating Virtual Asset Service Providers (VASP), providing a clear and comprehensive framework for their operations;
- ensuring compliance with stringent anti-money laundering (AML) and counter-terrorism financing rules, maintaining the integrity of the virtual asset ecosystem;
- protecting investors in the digital asset space, fostering confidence and trust in this emerging sector; and
- promoting innovation in blockchain and virtual assets, driving the development of this cutting-edge technology.

16. VARA's establishment reflects Dubai's proactive approach to regulating virtual assets, aiming to foster innovation while mitigating risks and protecting consumers.[19]

§ 6. CENTRAL BANK OF THE UAE

17. The Central Bank of the UAE plays a crucial role in maintaining the country's financial stability and overall economic health. Its key responsibilities include:

- formulating and implementing monetary policy, managing the currency, and controlling credit conditions;
- licensing and supervising banks and other financial institutions, ensuring their soundness and stability;
- enforcing AML regulations, combating financial crime, and protecting the integrity of the financial system; and
- overseeing payment systems and actively promoting the development of digital currencies, keeping the UAE at the forefront of financial innovation.

18. The Central Bank's role is pivotal in ensuring the stability and resilience of the UAE's financial system, which is crucial for attracting and retaining international investment.[20]

---

[19] VARA (ongoing), 'Virtual Assets Regulatory Authority', retrieved from https://www.vara.ae/.

[20] UAE Central Bank (ongoing), 'Central Bank of the UAE', retrieved from https://www.centralbank.ae/en/.

§ 7. INSURANCE AUTHORITY (NOW PART OF THE CENTRAL BANK)

19. The Insurance Authority, formerly a separate regulator, has been integrated into the Central Bank of the UAE, streamlining regulatory oversight of the insurance sector. It is responsible for:

- regulating insurance companies, reinsurance firms, insurance brokers, and agents, ensuring their financial stability and proper conduct; and
- overseeing consumer protection within the insurance sector, safeguarding the interests of policyholders and promoting fair practices.

20. This integration aims to enhance the efficiency and effectiveness of insurance sector regulation, further contributing to the stability of the UAE's financial system.[21]

SECTION IV. FUND PASSPORTING IN THE UAE

§ 1. GCC FUND PASSPORTING FRAMEWORK

21. A significant and recent development in the region's financial integration is the adoption of a fund passporting framework by the financial market authorities of the GCC. As announced by the Securities and Commodities Authority (SCA) in November 2024, this framework is designed to facilitate and streamline the cross-border offering of investment funds within the GCC, fostering greater regional cooperation. This initiative is a key step towards creating a more integrated and interconnected capital market in the Gulf region, promoting greater efficiency and attracting increased investment.[22]

§ 2. IMPORTANCE OF FUND PASSPORTING

22. Fund passporting is a mechanism that allows investment funds authorised in one jurisdiction to be offered to investors in other participating jurisdictions, subject to specific conditions and notifications. This initiative is expected to have a profound and transformative impact on the GCC financial landscape by:

---

[21] Ibid.

[22] SCA, 'GCC financial market authorities approve fund passporting framework', retrieved from https://www.sca.gov.ae/en/media-center/news/20/11/2024/gcc-financial-market-authorities-approve-fund-passporting-framework-with-implementation-scheduled.aspx.

- Enhancing Market Access: Fund managers will gain access to a broader and more diverse investor base across the GCC, significantly increasing their potential for growth and expansion.
- Boosting Regional Integration: The framework promotes greater integration of the GCC's financial markets, fostering stronger collaboration, deeper economic ties among Member States, and a more unified financial ecosystem.
- Increasing Efficiency: By streamlining and simplifying the process of offering funds across borders, passporting reduces regulatory burdens and costs, making it easier and more efficient for investors to diversify their portfolios and access a wider range of investment opportunities.
- Attracting International Investment: A more integrated, efficient, and dynamic GCC fund market is likely to attract greater interest from international investors seeking to capitalise on the region's growth potential and participate in its economic development.

23. The introduction of fund passporting is expected to significantly enhance the competitiveness of the GCC financial markets, making them more attractive to both regional and international investors.[23]

§ 3. IMPLEMENTATION

24. The GCC financial market authorities have officially approved the fund passporting framework, and implementation is proceeding according to the agreed-upon plan. This landmark initiative represents a significant step towards creating a more unified, interconnected, and dynamic financial market in the Gulf region, with far-reaching benefits for both investors and fund managers. The successful implementation of this framework will require close cooperation and coordination among the regulatory authorities of the GCC Member States.[24]

SECTION V. CONCLUSION

25. The UAE has firmly established itself as an exceptionally attractive jurisdiction for financial services, driven by a compelling combination of strategic factors and proactive policies. The country's embrace of the International Financial Centre model, exemplified by the remarkable success of ADGM and DIFC, has created a sophisticated and thriving ecosystem that effectively attracts

---

[23] Gulf Business, 'GCC fund passporting to boost regional investment', 2024, retrieved from https://gulfbusiness.com/gcc-fund-passporting-to-boost-regional-investment/.

[24] Zawya, 'GCC states to implement fund passporting framework', 2024, retrieved from https://www.zawya.com/en/legal/news/2024/02/29/gcc-states-to-implement-fund-passporting-framework-942685/.

global capital, top-tier talent, and cutting-edge innovation. The unique legal frameworks of these financial centres, particularly ADGM's direct application of UK common law, provide a level of certainty, stability, and predictability that is highly valued by international financial institutions seeking a secure and reliable base for their operations. Furthermore, recent ambitious initiatives like the GCC-wide fund passporting framework demonstrate the UAE's unwavering commitment to deepening regional financial integration, enhancing market access for investors and fund managers, and fostering a more interconnected and prosperous financial future for the region. As the global financial landscape continues to evolve rapidly, the UAE is exceptionally well-positioned to maintain its leadership role, serving as a vital bridge between East and West and a key driver of sustained economic growth and development in the Middle East and beyond. The UAE's strategic vision, combined with its commitment to regulatory excellence and innovation, positions it as a leading global financial centre for the years to come.[25]

[25] Emirates News Agency (ongoing), 'WAM', retrieved from https://wam.ae/.

PART 2.

UAE's Digital Dirham versus EU's Digital Euro Package

CHAPTER 1

CBDCS IN EMERGING MARKETS AND THE UAE'S DIGITAL DIRHAM EXAMPLE

Jack HARDMAN

SECTION I. INTRODUCTION

1. Clifford Chance provided a presentation on Central Bank Digital Currencies (CBDCs) for emerging markets and the UAE's 'Digital Dirham', which included a detailed overview of the potential impact and implementation of CBDCs in emerging markets and the public plans for the UAE.

2. This chapter covers the potential benefits and considerations for adopting CBDCs, focusing on emerging markets and practical factors and legal and regulatory frameworks. Whilst this chapter refers to certain international initiatives in these areas, we have not considered many of the complex macroeconomic issues with creating a CBDC, in particular those faced in jurisdictions such as the EU in adopting the digital euro.[1]

3. We then look at the characteristics of the Digital Dirham in the UAE and how the UAE federal legislation was amended to provide for the legislative basis and required characteristics for the Digital Dirham. We also cover considerations for the implementation of CBDCs in emerging markets.

SECTION II. CBDC AS A FUTURE OF MONEY – DOMESTICALLY

4. Clifford Chance noted how CBDC has the potential to transform the future of money and payments in emerging markets by addressing inefficiencies in legacy systems, improving payment efficiency, and facilitating technological innovations:

1 See T. BONNEAU, 'The Digital Euro Package of June 2023'.

- CBDC provides the ability to arrange 24/7 payment settlements, through recordation on a distributed ledger technology (DLT) platform. Other forms of digital payment transaction have typically relied upon bank-to-bank settlement mechanisms and clearing through the central bank's RTGS system, which occur when systems are available, which in some cases requires manual operations. Using CBDC allows transactions to be recorded automatically and instantaneously on a central digital platform through which all banks (and other regulated providers) can transact at all times. Consumers holding CBDC can also post their transactions to the system for instant 'atomic' settlement. In addition, as typically a private DLT/blockchain is controlled by the central bank, the surrounding regulatory and supervisory regime can be applied and the relevant mechanisms integrated with a secure central banking system. As such, CBDC can harness the benefits of using DLT/blockchain systems, in a similar way to settlement of crypto/virtual asset transfers, yet maintain the safety of taking place in a central bank system.
- As well as speed and continuous usage, the CBDC platform can drive cost efficiencies through reduced transaction fees by bypassing intermediary bank costs by direct transaction recording. Of course, intermediary banks will be required and this potential disintermediation is a major aspect to be considered in planning a successful CBDC, as detailed below.
- Technological innovations can arise through the use of money interests being recorded on such a digital platform. For example, the use of money can be preprogrammed by smart contracts created on the platform. This allows for features such as expiry dates and transaction limits to be built in. It also allows for certain CBDCs to be programmed for use in particular circumstances, such as for a specific transaction, time period, or the purchase of specific goods and services. This can create new use cases for CBDC. In the UAE, this could include methods of facilitating payments for expats, social and financial inclusion tools, and tourism use cases relevant to the local economy.
- More broadly, assuming a distributed ledger technology/blockchain is used, the CBDC platform would create a harmonised DLT platform to which relevant financial institutions could connect for payment transactions. We expect that the institutional adoption of such a platform would also spur further digital innovation as financial institutions and other participants can develop additional use cases, through smart contract development, for example. This platform could also be connected to permit atomic settlement of delivery vs. payment transactions with other digital assets, such as by use on future digital securities platforms.
- Finally, as highlighted below for the Digital Dirham, CBDC represents a direct claim on the central bank, eliminating credit risk on the banks. For a retail user, we do not expect this to be a determining factor in usage of CBDC

over a deposit,[2] but certain uses in the wholesale sector may find benefits from a lack of any counterparty credit risk for holdings. This is unlikely to outweigh the benefit of interest on such deposit holdings (where available). One potential use case would be for client money and escrow arrangements in jurisdictions where it is difficult to use a local bank account for client money due to limited depositor protection schemes, credit concerns on the bank or regulatory rules requiring client money to be held in an insolvency remote manner.

SECTION III. CBDC AS A TOOL FOR FINANCIAL INCLUSION IN EMERGING ECONOMIES

5. There is also a role for CBDC in increasing financial inclusion by providing digital payment access to those without traditional banking services. Many jurisdictions present challenges for certain sectors of the economy to hold bank accounts, for example by imposing a minimum salary requirement. Since users would be permitted to access the technology and create holdings in CBDC, it may not be necessary for such persons to hold traditional bank accounts, which such salary limits and other hurdles may prevent. This is of particular use in jurisdictions, such as the Gulf Cooperation Council (GCC), where there are a large number of low-paid migrant workers who are not able to set up a bank account, and who therefore seek a means of low-cost digital recording and transfers for cash.

SECTION IV. CBDC TO FACILITATE INTERNATIONAL TRANSFERS FOR REMITTANCE MARKETS

6. For international transfers, which are a key focus for the UAE, which has a majority expat population, the adoption of a CBDC network in one jurisdiction can also allow for interlinking with CBDC networks in other jurisdictions. The recently announced 'mBridge' platform[3] is one particular example already being set up. The mBridge project involves collaboration between the Bank of International Settlements (BIS) Innovation Hub, the Bank of Thailand, the UAE Central Bank, the Digital Currency Institute of the People's Bank of China, and the Hong Kong Monetary Authority. The Saudi Central Bank joined in 2024.[4]

2 Assuming there is general trust in the banking sector, and noting that, in some jurisdictions, there could be less trust on a claim against the central bank.

3 https://www.bis.org/about/bisih/topics/cbdc/mcbdc_bridge.htm.

4 See above.

The system would link the CBDC systems of the UAE, China, Hong Kong, and Thailand (as initial members) through a single transfer network allowing for instantaneous and low-cost transfers and exchange of currencies. Whilst such international platforms are likely to be rolled out at wholesale level initially, one can imagine a future where a person visiting one country can perform an instantaneous exchange of home currency to host currency to make a local payment by connection to an international CBDC transfer network.

SECTION V. CBDC AS AN OVERSIGHT TOOL

7. CBDCs provide central banks with greater oversight and control over payment transactions. By leveraging digital ledger technology, central banks can monitor transactions in real time, apply compliance tools, and implement measures to mitigate financial crime. This increased transparency helps in identifying and preventing illicit activities such as money laundering and terrorist financing.

SECTION VI. CASHLESS ECONOMY, BUT A NEED FOR TRUST

8. Building on the efficiencies noted above, the mass adoption of CBDC as a form of currency can further support a move to a cashless economy in developing economies, reducing expensive costs of managing physical currency and further reducing transaction frictions and costs. However, this requires a mindset change within sectors of society which prefer cash-based transactions. In particular, it requires individuals to give up the anonymity of cash in favour using a digital unit of payment which can be tracked and monitored by the state, further elaborated below.

SECTION VII. CBDC CHALLENGES AND USE-CASE-BASED ADOPTION

9. These benefits are, of course, not without their challenges.

10. In theory, CBDC usage may not need the involvement of a bank at all, given that (as described below) the CBDC represents a direct claim on the central bank. However, converting a central bank into a single state-wide bank for all retail account holders (including the responsibility to open accounts/wallets, conduct customer due diligence, oversee transactions, and other measures to avoid financial crime) is not realistic. Banks and other financial institutions will remain highly necessary for CBDC adoption, such that a successful roll-out of a CBDC programme will need to bring them along too.

11. The creation of CBDC involves a new form of holding money which is separate in nature from a traditional deposit and offers features which seek to avoid the involvement of traditional banking infrastructure in making payments and other transactions. Similar to the rise of fintech generally in recent years, this could disintermediate the banks through reduced reliance on bank accounts and traditional banking channels, which are revenue generating. Cross-selling of other products and services could also reduce if individuals are using a CBDC app (for example) to hold and transfer currency, rather than entering into the banking ecosystem.

12. Also, of course, if everyone used CBDC rather than traditional bank accounts, banks would not have access to the same level of retail deposits to fund their assets and the cost of funding could significantly increase, creating more expensive borrowing across the market and other macro-prudential impacts (see below).

13. Such financial institutions are, though, critical to the successful adoption of CBDC, as noted above. Therefore, it is likely to be necessary for the use of CBDC to focus on use-case-driven adoption sponsored by financial institutions, who can find new ways to allow customers to use their CBDC for specific means and, in the process, maintain customer relations alongside traditional deposits (as a mainstay) and cross-sell other products.

14. While the increased oversight from central banks can enhance security and compliance, it may also raise privacy concerns among the public. Individuals may worry about the extent of data collection and the potential misuse of their financial information. It is crucial for central banks to address these concerns by implementing robust data protection measures and ensuring transparency in their operations and usage of data.

15. Finally, adopting a DLT platform which will link to a central bank's core banking system to record currency transactions imports new software exposures. As a result, such emerging technologies bring cybersecurity risks. Jurisdictions adopting CBDCs will need to carefully ensure that robust controls are built around the CBDC network, and that there are sufficient experience and resources available. There have been high-profile hacks of central banks in the past, with disastrous effects.[5] Clearly, any risk of new technologies potentially opening up risks of cyberattacks needs to be closely managed.

---

5 The Bangladesh example is profiled at: https://www.isaca.org/resources/isaca-journal/issues/2023/volume-6/lessons-learned-from-the-bangladesh-bank-heist.

SECTION VIII. MACRO POLICY AND INTERNATIONAL INITIATIVES

16. There are a number of international organisations focused on these issues. However, such organisations are also considering the macro-prudential impacts of CBDC, which are beyond the scope of this chapter.

17. For instance, the IMF's CBDC Virtual Handbook is designed to be a reference guide for policymakers and experts at central banks and ministries of finance seeking to evaluate CBDCs.[6] According to its site, this handbook aims to collect and share knowledge, lessons, empirical findings, and frameworks to address policymakers' most frequently asked questions on CBDCs. Importantly, the chapters cover impacts on financial stability and monetary policy, not referred to above.

18. The BIS has also published numerous papers on the foundational principles and core features of CBDCs, including financial stability implications. Importantly, the BIS has surveyed and identified that the vast majority of global central banks are looking into CBDCs and their implications, with many live projects.[7]

19. Of final mention, the World Economic Forum's Digital Currency Governance Consortium, including its White Paper Series, discusses the benefits and considerations for CBDC, seeking to raise global awareness of the opportunities, challenges, and risks posed by new forms of digital currency.[8]

SECTION IX. CONCLUSIONS ON CBDC ADOPTION

20. Noting the factors above, exploring CBDCs in emerging markets is a significant undertaking that involves complex decisions in a rapidly changing digital environment, with many competing digital payments initiatives. Along with developing the technology to allow CBDC and the core prudential measures and financial arrangements within the central bank, a number of key considerations will be required concurrently, including:

- Jurisdictions must clearly establish the policy objectives of CBDCs and relevant success measures, including whether the intention is mass adoption,

---

6 https://www.imf.org/en/Topics/digital-payments-and-finance/central-bank-digital-currency/virtual-handbook.

7 https://www.bis.org/publ/bppdf/bispap147.htm. See T. Bonneau, 'The Digital Euro Package of June 2023'.

8 https://www.weforum.org/communities/digital-currency-governance-consortium/

a societal use-case-driven approach, or to allow the availability of such new technologies.

- Risks must be identified, quantified as much as possible, and accompanied by a strategy to contain them. Domestic authorities should undertake a careful assessment of their capacity to experiment with, regulate, oversee, and eventually implement CBDCs.
- Communication about CBDCs with relevant stakeholders and the general population is important to support the intended form of adoption, noting the need, mentioned above, to have the banks on board.
- Finally, a sound legal basis and robust regulatory foundations should underpin the CBDC project from the start, which is covered in the following sections focusing on the UAE's Digital Dirham.

SECTION X. DIGITAL DIRHAM PROPERTIES

21. The Digital Dirham in the UAE is intended to operate as a form of currency and legal tender in its own right, meaning that it can be legally used to extinguish a debt.

22. It is to be distinguished from a deposit (being a claim on a bank; that is, a debt owed by the bank) in that CBDC is a direct claim on the central bank. As noted above, this theoretically reduces the need for holdings with a bank in traditional form. However, in practice, we expect the adoption of the Digital Dirham to operate through wallets opened with a customer's bank (which would have conducted the relevant KYC/CDD and transaction oversight noted above).

23. It will exists as a virtual asset recorded on a distributed ledger technology (DLT), which shall be a private and permissioned system.

24. As such, it was important to ensure that the legislative framework was adapted to reflect the required legal status of the Digital Dirham. Clifford Chance was chosen by the UAE Central Bank to support the development of the legal framework outlined in the following sections.

SECTION XI. LEGISLATIVE APPROACH

25. Legislative changes are generally required to establish a legal basis for digital currencies. Amendments may be needed to clarify the central bank's powers to issue and to grant legal tender status to CBDC. Amendments to traditional central bank laws will likely be needed where such laws only anticipate cash in the form of notes and coins, to allow for digital equivalents, including laws which relate to defacing currency – how should that work for CBDC?

26. Other laws outside of banking legislation will need to recognise digital currency as lawful tender, especially where terms like 'currency' and 'cash' are used in legislation. Finally, depending on the form of adoption, banking laws pertaining to the recognition and operation of transfer systems and recognition of central bank holdings may need to be updated to reflect systems for the holdings and transfers of CBDC. These changes would ensure that CBDCs are legally recognised and can be used in everyday transactions, and permit the proposed use cases. Benchmarks across the world offer useful insights for jurisdictions to consider, along with international guidance such as the references highlighted above.

27. However, in general, benchmarks need to be carefully considered, especially for emerging markets. Many changes to a jurisdiction's legislative framework will require specific amendments particular to that jurisdiction, given that traditional provisions around currency have often been designed in different ways. We had noted significant variance in the legislative approach in emerging markets, often reflecting the nascent adoption of CBDCs in many jurisdictions and limited examples of mass adoption. Generally, however, legislation in emerging markets has taken a principles-based and limited approach to amending its law.

28. Also, the nature of the legal framework for central banks will determine the legal amendments to adopt. Many emerging jurisdictions have a central bank law which dictates matters of currency and may require amendment. Other jurisdictions may deal with currency matters across multiple implementing laws or permit matters of currency to be covered in subordinate legislation. In general, multiple laws will need to be considered, including laws on data privacy and cyber offences, as noted below.

29. In the UAE, the Central Bank Law is a federal law, which may take precedence over other laws, and which allows amendments to this specific law for CBDC, which took place in 2023 . Amendments necessary for CBDC were made, adopting technologically neutral terms, where appropriate, to permit flexibility.

SECTION XII. CASE STUDY – AMENDMENTS TO THE UAE CENTRAL BANK LAW

30. As noted above, in 2023, the UAE Central Bank law was amended[9] to accommodate the issuance and regulation of currency in digital form. This includes provisions for the creation of digital currency, its legal tender status,

[9] UAE Decretal Federal Law (54) of 2023.

transfers and holdings, recognition across UAE laws, and provisions for the regulatory framework for its use. Key amendments made are detailed as follows:

- **'Currency' definition**: The definition of currency was amended to include currency in digital form, in addition to notes and coins, ensuring clarity and legal recognition.
- **Currency issuance**: New articles were also added to govern the issuance of digital currency, supplementing existing provisions for notes and coins, ensuring the power of the Central Bank to issue the Digital Dirham as an official currency.
- **Currency specifications and features**: Additional amendments permit the Central Bank to issue the digital currency with specific denominations, designs, and features. This, importantly, ensures that the Central Bank can clarify the relevant features of the CBDC in its issuance decision, and will include matters such as possession arrangements for distribution.
- **Legal tender force**: Amendments ensure that legal tender status is afforded to the digital form of currency, to be recognised as a valid form of payment.
- **Penalties, including cyber considerations**: Like other traditional laws which cover currency notes and coins, laws restrict mutilation or shredding of such forms of cash. The law was clarified to ensure that digital currency would be covered, to capture unlawful destruction of CBDC. However, in the realm of a digital currency recorded on a DLT platform, damage to the CBDC, as well as its relevant network, will need to be considered. The UAE, amongst other jurisdictions, has a comprehensive cybercrimes framework which covers hacking and related unlawful acts in respect of a digital network, and this will extend to the Digital Dirham system.
- **Monetary base coverage**: An amendment was made to ensure that the Central Bank can hold foreign digital currencies as part of its reserves, which may be necessary for international transactions and engagement with international platforms for CBDC exchange.
- **Opening of accounts**: An amendment was made to allow the Central Bank to open accounts or other holdings of currency in digital form. Noting that CBDCs can be account- or token-based, the amendment permits the Central Bank to maintain other forms of digital currency financial balances, whatever their type.
- **'Transfer Order' definition**: The definition of 'Transfer Order' was amended to clarify the treatment of digital currency transfers in financial infrastructure systems. This definition is used to denote the transfer transactions which a recognised financial infrastructure system may clear/settle. The definition was amended such that transactions which put funds in the control of a participant on such a system would be a 'Transfer Order', reflecting the nature of certain digital asset transactions.
- **Interpretation of UAE laws to include Digital Dirham**: As noted above, there are many other laws which refer to 'cash' and 'money', and such laws should

recognise that such terms would include currency in digital form, to ensure that Digital Dirham has the appropriate recognition UAE-wide. As such, an interpretative article was included such that references to 'cash' and 'money' in other laws include digital currency. The law also specifies that digital forms of currency are not considered virtual assets.

SECTION XIII. IMPLEMENTING REQUIREMENTS

31. There are likely to be several legal requirements for implementing a CBDC platform in emerging markets, including rules for financial institutions, regulations at the customer level, and use-case-supporting measures.

32. Many of these requirements may leverage existing regulatory frameworks. However, the implementing regulations may also need to cover novel topics, such as the use of programmable money, smart contracts, and the institutionalisation of digital assets through integration with DLT platforms.

33. It will need to be considered whether the methods of CBDC distribution, and the entities permitted to do this, may give rise to new types of regulated activities and new entities, such as fintechs supporting development and distribution, which may need to be licensed.

34. Implementing measures may also need to address issues such as extending the AML regime, consumer protection, and data privacy, depending on the method of adoption. If the adoption of the CBDC is made mandatory for certain sectors, one particular area of concern may be to adopt a proportionate approach to any requirements for small merchants and fintech providers, who may not have the resources to develop tools and systems to support acceptance/processing of CBDC transactions. This is a feature of the digital euro proposals.

35. Overall, the legislative and regulatory regime for the successful adoption and roll-out of CBDC in emerging markets does not end with the central bank law itself. Whilst the central bank laws may function to permit a CBDC and grant core requirements – as demonstrated by the detailed legislative proposal supporting the digital euro – significant additional implementing measures may be required for successful implementation.

La Sorbonne AD, 20 February 2025

CHAPTER 2
THE DIGITAL EURO PACKAGE OF JUNE 2023

Thierry BONNEAU

1. The year 2023 was marked by the publication of the Crypto Assets Regulation – it is a 31 May 2023 regulation[1] – and by the publication, on 28 June 2023, of a proposal concerning the digital euro.[2] As the latter is 'analysed as a crypto-asset", one might assume that it is subject to the 31 May 2023 regulation. However, this is not the case, as the regulation does not apply to the European Central Bank (ECB).[3]

2. This proposal is part of one of the two packages published on 28 June 2023. The first concerns financial data[4] and payment services.[5] The second concerns the 'single currency'. The proposals about payment services – a proposal for a regulation and a proposal for a directive – are partly connected to the second package because they take into account the plan to establish the digital euro.

---

1 Regulation (EU) 2023/1114 of the European Parliament and of the Council of 31 May 2023 on markets in crypto-assets, and amending Regulations (EU) No. 1093/2010 and (EU) No. 1095/2010 and Directives 2013/36/EU and (EU) 2019/1937. See T. BONNEAU, *Le règlement MICA du 31 mai 2023, Revue de Droit Bancaire et financier* 2023, No. 14; T. BONNEAU, *Régulation bancaire et financière européenne et internationale*, Bruylant 7 2024, no. 506.21 *et seq.*

2 Proposal for a Regulation of the European Parliament and of the Council establishing the digital euro, COM(2023) 369 final, 28 June 2023. See T. BONNEAU and P. STORRER, *L'euro numérique et les concepts associés dans ls propositions du 28 juin 2023*, RISF 2023/4, p. 14.

3 Art. 2, MICA Regulation: '2. This Regulation does not apply to: ... (c) the ECB, central banks of the Member States when acting in their capacity as monetary authorities, or other public authorities of the Member States'.

4 Proposal for a Regulation of the European Parliament and of the Council concerning the framework for access to financial data and amending Regulations (EU) No. 1093/2010, (EU) No. 1094/2010 (EU), No. 1095/2010 and (EU) 2022/2554, COM (2003) 360 final, 28 June 2023.

5 Proposal for a Directive of the European Parliament and of the Council on payment services and electronic money services in the internal market, amending Directive 98/26/EC and repealing Directives (EU) 2015/2366 and 2009/110/EC, COM (2023) 366 final, 28 June 2023; Proposal for a Regulation of the European Parliament and of the Council on payment services in the internal market and amending Regulation (EU) No. 1093/2010.

3. The package on the single currency contains three proposals for regulations: the first proposal concerns the legal tender status of euro banknotes and coins ('Proposal 364');[6] the second concerns the establishment of the digital euro ('Proposal 369');[7] the third aims to enable payment service providers ('PSPs') from countries whose currency is not the euro to be in a position to distribute this new form of the euro ('Proposal 368').[8]

4. These proposals have been published even though there is a certain amount of scepticism among the public, in particular because customers may think that they are already 'using a form of digital euro when they pay with their bank card or mobile phone', and because there are fears that the digital euro, due to its lack of anonymity, could be a means of 'controlling individual spending'.[9] I should add that credit institutions are worried that the scriptural money deposits they rely on to grant loans will be siphoned off by the digital euro.[10] We understand, however, that the proposals are in some way a response to threats from the tech world, and that the digital euro is 'an opportunity for Europe to preserve its monetary sovereignty'.[11] This is not what Donald Trump, the president of the United States, thinks.[12]

5. Proposal 368 may seem anecdotal in view of the entities involved, but it should not be overlooked and is necessary, given that not all European Union ('EU') Member States have adopted the euro as their currency. Proposal 364 does not concern the digital euro, but it is not without importance as it takes a stand on the concept of legal tender for euro banknotes and coins, a comparable objective to that being pursued by Proposal 369, which aims to establish the digital euro.

6. Proposal 364 is made up of 17 articles. There are no chapters. Proposal 369 comprises 42 articles divided into 10 chapters, entitled 'Subject matter and definitions' (Chapter 1), 'Establishing and issuance of the digital EU euro' (Chapter 2), 'Legal tender' (Chapter 3), 'Distribution' (Chapter 4), 'Use of the digital euro as a store of value and as a means of payment' (Chapter 5),

---

6 Proposal for a Regulation of the European Parliament and of the Council on the legal tender status of euro banknotes and coins, COM (2023) 364 final, 28 June 2023.

7 Proposal for a Regulation establishing the digital euro, above, n. 2.

8 Proposal for a Regulation of the European Parliament and of the Council on the provision of digital euro services by payment service providers established in Member States whose currency is not the euro and amending Regulation (EU) 2021/1230 of the European Parliament and of the Council, COM (2023) 368 final, 28 June 2023.

9 F. Collomp and D. Guinot, 'L'euro numérique avance, le scepticisme persiste', *Figaro*, 17 October 2023.

10 M. Heilmann, 'Le projet d'euro numérique de la BCE entre dans le vif du sujet', *Les Echos*, 2 December 2024.

11 F. Collomp and D. Guinot, above n. 9.

12 E. Lefevre, 'Trumps met son véto au développement d'une monnaie numérique par la Fed', *Les Echos*, 23 January 2025.

'Distribution of the digital euro outside the euro area' (Chapter 6), 'Technical features' (Chapter 7), 'Privacy and data protection' (Chapter 8), 'Anti-money laundering' (Chapter 9), and 'Final provisions' (Chapter 10).

7. I will try to address the package in three sections. The first section aims to situate the digital euro in relation to the single currency (I). The second looks at the digital euro from the point of view of stakeholders, whether central banks, customers, or professionals (II). In addition to these two sections, I would like to add a third which concerns the implementation of the digital euro. The purpose of this section is to highlight some of the difficulties and problems associated with the digital euro (III).

SECTION I. THE DIGITAL EURO AND THE SINGLE CURRENCY

8. The digital euro is not a new currency, but only a new form of the single currency. Like coins and banknotes, the digital euro is legal tender. The digital euro is not without links with the other forms of the single currency.

§ 1. A NEW FORM OF THE SINGLE CURRENCY

9. The digital euro is not a new currency, but a new form of the single currency. Article 3 of Proposal 369 bears witness to this: 'The digital euro is established as a digital form of the single currency.' Echoing this, the proposals for PSD[13] 3 and the Payment Services Regulation redefine the concept of 'funds', which now comprises 'central bank money issued for retail use, scriptural money and electronic money'.[14]

§ 2. LEGAL TENDER FOR DIGITAL CURRENCY

10. The concept of legal tender[15] was created for coins (metallic money) and banknotes (fiduciary money). It does not apply to scriptural money, which is

---

13 PSD: Payement services directive.

14 Art. 3(30), Proposal for a regulation on payment services in the internal market, above n. 5.

15 See T. Bonneau, 'The concept of legal tender in France' in R. Freitag and S. Omlor (eds), *The Euro as Legal Tender: A Comparative Approach to a Uniform Concept*, Berlin, De Gruyter, 2020, pp. 79 *et seq.*

regarded a claim on credit institutions, whereas metallic and fiduciary money are claims on the central bank.[16]

11. For a long time, there was no legal definition of the concept of legal tender. No definition was given by EU law. There was only a Commission Recommendation[17] emphasising that legal tender for euro banknotes and coins should imply compulsory acceptance, acceptance at face value, and the power to discharge. It was only a ruling by the ECJ on 26 January 2021[18] that gave a definition for euro banknotes and coins: 'the notion of "legal tender" of a means of payment denominated in a monetary unit means, in its current sense, that this means of payment cannot generally be refused in settlement of a debt denominated in the same monetary unit, at its face value, with full discharge effect'.[19] This definition was taken up by Proposals 364 and 369 of the regulation of 28 June 2023.

12. According to Article 4 of Proposal 364, the legal tender status of cash – banknotes and coins – is defined by the following three rules: their compulsory acceptance, at their face value, and with the power to discharge. These terms are explained in Article 4:

2. In accordance with the principle of compulsory acceptance of cash, the beneficiary shall not refuse euro notes and/or coins presented in payment to satisfy a payment obligation.
3. In accordance with the principle of acceptance of cash at face value, the monetary value of the euro notes and/or coins presented to settle a debt is equal to the amount in euros indicated on the notes and/or coins. Additional charges for settling a debt with euro notes and coins are prohibited.
4. In accordance with the power of discharge, a payer may discharge a payment obligation by presenting euro banknotes and coins to the payee.

13. This text is echoed in Article 7 of Proposal 369, which states that 'the digital euro is legal tender'. The Article explains the attributes of legal tender for the digital euro in a similar way to Article 4 of Proposal 364:

- the legal tender status of the digital euro implies its compulsory acceptance, at its nominal value, as a means of payment with the power to discharge obligations;

---

16 See C. Kleiner, 'Monnaie et paiement: du mérite de l'innovation technologique au grand chambardement légistique' in *Chronique de droit bancaire international 2023, Revue Dr. Bancaire et financier* September–October 2023, 3, no. 12 *et seq.*, spec. no. 21.

17 Commission Recommendation of 22 March 2010 on the scope and effects of legal tender for euro banknotes and coins.

18 Joined Cases C-422/19 and C-423/19, *Hessischer Rundfunk*, ECLI:EU:C:2021:63.

19 Ibid., point 46.

- by virtue of the obligation to accept the digital euro, the beneficiary of a payment obligation may not refuse digital euros presented to comply with the obligation;
- under the obligation to accept the digital euro at its face value, the monetary value of digital euros presented in settlement of a debt is equal to the value of the pecuniary debt. The imposition of additional charges for the payment of a debt made in digital euros is prohibited; and
- by virtue of the dischargeability of the digital euro, a payer may discharge a payment obligation by presenting digital euros to the payee.

14. Legal tender is a different concept from the notion of 'forced money' *(cours forcé)*. The latter notion covers the dispensation of central banks from having to pay back the banknotes in gold.[20] The phrase 'forced money' is, in fact, equivalent to the term 'inconvertibility'. However, the distinction is not so obvious because, for some, legal tender is called 'forced money' when it is applied to inconvertible paper money.[21]

15. The approach followed by the EU proposals raises several questions.

16. Firstly, we might ask why there is not just one text; why are two texts needed? Could the concept not have been defined once, and therefore in a single text?

17. Secondly, the concept is linked solely to the issuer of the currency.[22] This is reasonable since it applies to coins and banknotes as well as to the digital euro. However, it is surprising that scriptural money has been excluded, because money creation by banks is based on the monetary policy of the central bank, and because scriptural money is expressed in euros. The euro is a single currency, regardless of its denomination or material support.

18. Thirdly, should we link the legal tender to the currency or to the support? It could be claimed that the currency itself does not have any specific value because it cannot be paid back in gold. This position would explain that the legal tender is linked to the form of the euro. However, it could be argued that, despite the fact that it cannot be paid back in gold, the euro has a value: a value connected to the economy of countries whose currency is the euro. Consequently, the reasoning based on the absence of the notion of forced money is not convincing.

19. Finally, is the concept of legal tender appropriate for digital money? In other words, is it so protean that it can be adapted to any monetary medium?[23]

---

[20] F. Grua and N. Cayrol, *Régime général des obligations – Paiement des obligations de somme d'argent – Monnaie de paiement, Juris-classeur civil code*, Art. 1343 to 1343-5, fasc. 30 (2017) no. 4.

[21] *Répétitions écrites sur les Monnaies, Crédit et Change, Les cours de droit* (1938–1939) 22.

[22] C. Kleiner, 'Monnaie et paiement', above n. 15, no. 21.

[23] Ibid.

§ 3. INTERACTION BETWEEN EURO BANKNOTES AND COINS AND THE DIGITAL EURO

20. The physical and digital forms of the single currency are of equal importance.[24] The digital euro will be convertible at parity with euro banknotes and coins.[25] The digital euro will also be convertible at parity with scriptural money and electronic money denominated in euros.[26]

21. The acceptance of digital euro payments is independent of cash payments, each obeying their own rules.[27] As far as the settlement of a pecuniary debt is concerned, it has been decided that:

> Payees of a pecuniary debt denominated in euro shall accept payments in euro banknotes and coins in accordance with the provisions of this Regulation, whether or not they accept payments in digital euro in accordance with Regulation [(EU) XXX/XXX establishing the digital euro]. Where the acceptance of euro banknotes and coins and the digital euro is mandatory in accordance with the provisions of this Regulation and Regulation [(EU) XXX/XXX establishing the digital euro], the payer shall have the right to choose the means of payment.[28]

SECTION II. THE DIGITAL EURO AND STAKEHOLDERS

22. Central banks are at the basis of the digital euro. The success of its establishment requires us to define to what extent customers may use the digital euro, and the duties on professionals responsible for its distribution.

§ 1. CENTRAL BANKS

23. The fact that the digital euro is a new form of the single currency is not without consequence: it naturally requires the ECB and the national central banks to have a monopoly on issuance and 'direct liability' towards digital euro users.[29]

---

24 Recital 6, Proposal 369, above n. 2.
25 Art. 15(1), Proposal 364, above n. 6; Art. 12(1), Proposal 369, above n. 2.
26 Art. 13(5), Proposal 369, above n 2.
27 Ibid., Art. 12(2)2, Proposal 369.
28 Art. 15(2), Proposal 364, above n. 6.
29 Art. 4(2), Proposal 369, above n. 2.

§ 2. CLIENTS

24. Customers will be able to hold payment accounts in digital euros and payment accounts in 'non-digital euros'. These two types of account will coexist, without the opening of a digital euro account being subject to the opening of a non-digital euro account: 'In their relationship with their payment service providers for the provision of digital euro payment services, digital euro users are not required to hold or open non-digital euro payment accounts or to accept other non-digital euro products.'[30] It should be noted, at the same time, that digital euro accounts can be linked to non-digital euro accounts.[31]

25. The digital euro may be used as a means of payment.[32] It must 'be available for both online and offline digital payment transactions'. [33] It is indicated that 'the digital euro, held online or offline, shall be convertible at par between each other, at the request of digital euro users' .[34]

26. The digital euro can also be used as a store of value. A certain number of limits are imposed on the use of the digital euro as a store of value, in accordance with monetary policy and in order to contribute to the stability of the financial system.[35] Rules are laid down to prevent excessive charges, so that the digital euro can be used effectively as legal tender.[36]

27. The digital euro must be accessible to all clients. Article 22, paragraph 1, of Proposal 369 attests to this. According to this text:

> [T]he digital euro shall:
>
> a) have usage and service features that are simple and easy to handle, including for people with disabilities or functional limitations or with limited digital skills and older persons;
>
> b) be accessible for persons with disabilities by complying with the accessibility requirements laid down in Annex 1 of Directive 2019/882.[37]

---

30 Ibid., Art. 22(2).
31 Ibid., Art. 22(4).
32 Ibid., Art. 15(1), Art. 16.
33 Ibid., Art. 23(1).
34 Ibid., Art. 23(2).
35 Ibid., Art. 15(1), Art. 16.
36 Ibid., Art. 15(2), Art. 17.
37 Directive (EU) 2019/882 of the European Parliament and of the Council of 17 April 2019 on accessibility requirements for products and services.

§ 3. PROFESSIONALS

28. The digital euro will be distributed by payment service providers (PSPs) incorporated in Member States whose currency is the euro,[38] and by those incorporated in Member States whose currency is not the euro.[39] The aim is for all EU PSPs to have the right to distribute digital euro payment services in the eurozone.

29. Payment service providers will make available funding and defunding functionalities to digital euro users.[40] Proposal 369 explains the concepts of funding and defunding:

- 'funding' means the process whereby a digital euro user acquires digital euros, in exchange for either cash or other funds, creating a direct liability of the ECB or a national central bank towards that digital euro user;[41]
- 'defunding' means the process whereby a digital euro user exchanges digital euro with cash or other funds.[42]

30. On this occasion, payment services are transformed into 'digital euro payment services', as listed in Annex I of the proposed regulation.[43] Similarly, and just as curiously, the concepts of 'digital euro payment transactions',[44] 'digital euro payment account'[45], etc. appear.

31. A sort of 'second law' for payment services 'in' digital euros is thus emerging, which, at least at this stage, continues to amaze. This duality is confirmed by the definitions of payment transactions[46] and payment accounts[47] given in the proposal for a regulation on payment services. However, there is

---

38 Art. 13 *et seq.*, Proposal 369, above n. 2.

39 Proposal 368, above n. 8.

40 Art. 13(3), Proposal 369, above n. 2.

41 Ibid., Art. 2(11).

42 Ibid., Art. 2(12).

43 Ibid., Recital 6.

44 Ibid., Art. 2(3): '"digital euro payment transaction" means an act, initiated by a payer or on his or her behalf, or by the payee, of placing, transferring or withdrawing digital euro, irrespective of any underlying obligations between the payer and the payee.'

45 Ibid., Art. 2(5: '"digital euro payment account" means an account held by one or more digital euro users with a payment service provider to access digital euro recorded in the digital euro settlement infrastructure or in an offline digital euro device and to initiate or receive digital euro payment transactions, whether offline or online, and irrespective of technology and data structure.'

46 Art. 3(5), Proposal 367: '"payment transaction" means an act of placing, transferring or withdrawing funds, based on a payment order placed by the payer, or on his behalf, or by the payee, or on his behalf, irrespective of any underlying obligations between the payer and the payee.'

47 Ibid., Art. 3(15), Proposal 367: '"payment account" means an account held by a payment service provider in the name of one or more payment service users which is used for the execution of one or more payment transactions and allows for sending and receiving funds to and from third parties.'

some overlap because of the definition given to the term 'funds',[48] which includes central bank money issued for retail use, which was intended to include the digital euro.

32. This duality raises questions. One wonders whether the obligations of entities distributing the digital euro will be subject solely to the regulation establishing the digital euro or whether PSD 2, and in the future PSD 3, will also apply to them. This is a significant issue for customers, who are protected by the PSDs in the event of a dispute. The introduction of a 'second law' on payment services might suggest that the law on payment services (PSD 2/PSD 3) is not applicable. But this conclusion is hasty and is contradicted by Article 4, section 2 of proposed Regulation 368:

> In accordance with Article 4(25) of Directive (EU) 2015/2366 of the European Parliament and of the Council, of 25 November 2015, on payment services in the internal market, as amended by Directive (EU) [please insert reference – proposal for a Directive on payment services and electronic money services in the internal market - COM/2023/366 final], the provisions of that Directive shall apply to payment transactions in digital euro.

However, Proposal 366 does not amend PSD 2 but repeals it and replaces it with a new text, and the reference to a text defining the word 'funds'[49] does not seem very useful for determining the application of a text.

SECTION III. THE IMPLEMENTATION OF THE DIGITAL EURO

33. Implementing the digital euro is a vast undertaking. It was the subject of a two-year investigation phase prior to publication of the 2023 package. In October 2023, the ECB launched a preparatory phase for the project, which is due to last until October 2025. At that point, the legislative process should be complete, at which point the ECB will decide whether or not to launch the digital euro. It is not expected to become a reality until 2028.[50]

---

48 Art. 3(30), Proposal for a Regulation of the European Parliament and of the Council on payment services in the internal market and amending Regulation (EU) No. 1093/2010: '"funds" means central bank money issued for retail use, scriptural money and electronic money.'

49 See above, n. 24 and n. 26.

50 M. Heilmann, above n. 10, spec. question 15.

§ 1. TECHNICAL INFRASTRUCTURE

34. Implementing the digital euro requires technical infrastructure. This raises the question of who can provide this. Is it public entities, such as national central banks, or private players? If the latter, do they have to be European, or can they be non-European, such as American? But does this not raise privacy concerns?

§ 2. PRIVACY AND PERSONAL DATA

35. The question of privacy is very important because the use of the digital euro may leave traces. The ECB is reassuring. The digital euro is designed to protect privacy. Offline payments would have a level of protection comparable to that of cash: only payers and payees would have access to payment information. For online payments, there will be strict rules and controls to prevent the identification of individuals: data will be anonymised. It should be noted, however, that credit institutions will have access to the personal data they need to comply with EU law, particularly with regard to money laundering.[51]

§ 3. HOW WOULD THE DIGITAL EURO WORK?

36. These assurances should encourage individuals to use the digital euro in shops or online, regardless of the country in the eurozone or the payment service provider. The question is, however, how the digital euro can work in practice.

37. It could be based on the creation of a digital euro wallet that could be fed from a bank account.[52] As we understand it, customers would be able to transfer digital euros from one wallet to another, but for the moment it is not clear how this transfer would work when it takes place offline, in particular at a retailer or between friends, and without any trace in a bank account, which would be the case if the transfer were made using a bank card linked to a digital euro account. But perhaps the difficulty should not be exaggerated. It was pointed out that direct wallet-to-wallet payments could be made via a phone or a watch, in a similar way to a cash payment.[53]

---

[51] BCE, *Foire aux questions sur un euro numérique*, 16 juillet 2025,., spec. question 9 *et pour en savoir plus: Euro numérique et vie privée.*

[52] Ibid, spec. question 7 *et pour en savoir plus: comment un euro numérique fonctionnerait-il?*

[53] BCE, *Foire aux questions sur un euro numérique, quesiton 7, Comment un euro numérique fonctionnerait-il?*, op. cit.

§ 4. INTERNATIONAL PAYMENTS

38. Wallet-to-wallet payments or payments online can be made not only within the EU but also in third countries. And, as the EU is made up of 27 countries, payments between a client domiciled in France, for example, and another in Germany, will be cross-border payments, which are treated in the same way as national payments under European legislation.[54] They are international payments if one of the payer or the payee is located in the EU and the other is in a third country. By hypothesis, the payment is made in euros to the beneficiary located in a third country.

39. Insofar as the digital euro is only one form of the euro, it may be thought that a payment in digital euros should be treated the same as a payment in non-digital euros. Hence, the classic question of whether a payment can be made in a foreign currency arises in the same way for the non-digital euro as for the digital euro. More specifically, the question is whether a third country accepts payment in euros. We know that, in France, a distinction is made according to whether the contract is domestic or international. In the first case, the foreign currency can only be a unit of account, and the currency of payment must be the euro. In the second case, the foreign currency can be both a currency of account and a currency of payment.[55]

40. Another question must be raised. Again, by hypothesis, the payee has an account in a third country. We need to see whether it is possible for this beneficiary to hold a digital euro account in that country. This depends on the legislation of that country, which explains the approach adopted by the ECB, which considers only individuals, companies, and organisations that reside in or are established temporarily or permanently in a eurozone country.

SECTION IV. CONCLUSION

41. We could ask many more questions. In particular, in some countries, it is prohibited to pay in cash above a certain amount. Does this ban apply to digital euro payments? It was pointed out that the digital euro proposals do not address these issues, in particular private international law.[56] But, of course, these proposals are still just plans and all the issues are undoubtedly under discussion.

---

[54] C. Kleiner, *Les conflits de lois soulevés par un paiement international en monnaies numériques de banque centrale* (MNBC), RISF 2023/4, pp. 19 *et seq.*, spec. p. 21.

[55] T. Bonneau, *Droit bancaire*, 15th ed., Paris, LGDJ, 2023, no. 702. See also C. Kleiner, *Les conflits*, above n. 53, spec. p. 22.

[56] C. Kleiner, *Les conflits*, above n. 53.

PART 3.

What Model for Regulating Crypto-Assets?

TITLE 1
TAXONOMY OF CRYPTO-ASSETS

CHAPTER 1

THE MICA REGULATION METHODOLOGY: STRENGTH AND LIMITS

Pauline PAILLER

1. The European MiCA regulation[1] reflects the European Union (EU)'s legal policy choice regarding crypto-assets. The EU had to decide which regulatory model to favour for these new assets, which are specific in that they are registered on a blockchain, 'tokenised'. The first question that arises is how to define a crypto-asset: should the definition be based on form or substance (that is to say, on the substance of the rights that the crypto-asset confers)? The second question concerns the regime: should crypto-assets be subject to a new regime, specially created by the policymaker, or should they be subject to a pre-existing regime? The latter could be the financial instruments regime, given that such instruments mostly serve the same investment and speculative purposes, and are subject to mandatory regulation in Europe, as in many other countries.

2. Following previous models from Member States, particularly France,[2] the European lawmaker (that is to say, the European Council, the European Commission, and the European Parliament) has decided to regulate crypto-assets through the MiCA Regulation, a specific regulation on crypto-asset markets. This new regulation seems straightforward, as it suggests that the European policymaker has opted for a new regime based on a purely formal criterion: the registration on a blockchain. However, as we shall see, things are more complicated in reality because the MiCA Regulation also considers the substance of the asset and, to a certain extent, leaves room for pre-existing regimes, such as that for financial markets or, as far as stablecoins are concerned, that for electronic money or e-money.

3. Therefore, at first glance, it seems that the European lawmaker has opted for a specific regulatory model for crypto-assets (the MiCA Regulation), that excludes the pre-existing ones (particularly the public policy regulation of

---

1 Regulation (EU) 2023/1114 of 31 May 2023 on crypto-asset markets (MiCA Regulation).

2 See Law no. 2019-486 of 22 May 2019 (known as PACTE Law).

financial market law[3] and of e-money[4]). However, the method is far from being so simple and binary. In fact, some crypto-assets, such as security tokens, confer the same financial and/or political rights as financial instruments. The conclusions are the same concerning stablecoins, which can fit into the category of e-money. In the event of overlapping qualifications – in other words, if a crypto-asset is also a financial instrument or an e-money – the MiCA Regulation takes a back seat to make way for the regulations applicable to financial instruments or e-money. This is to prevent financial instruments from being registered on a blockchain merely in order to circumvent the applicable financial markets regulations.

4. However, this choice poses a number of difficulties that the MICA Regulation struggles to overcome. While the European lawmaker sets out several methodological principles intended to facilitate the articulation of the different regulations (I), the method reveals some weaknesses at the application stage (II).

SECTION I. THE ARTICULATION METHOD

5. The MiCA Regulation establishes a method in order to articulate the concepts of crypto-assets and other assets, based on three key principles: first, a technical and non-legal definition of crypto-assets (1); second, a principle of technological neutrality (2); and, third, an open-ended typology of crypto-assets (3).

§ 1. A TECHNICAL DEFINITION OF A CRYPTO-ASSET

6. The first element is the MiCA Regulation's definition of a crypto-asset. A crypto-asset is defined as 'a digital representation of a value or right that can be transferred and stored electronically using distributed ledger or similar technology'.[5] The defining criterion for a crypto-asset is its digital representation: it is registered on a blockchain, enabling it to be stored and transferred. In this

---

3 In particular, Directive 2014/65/EU of the European Parliament and of the Council of 15 May 2014 on markets in financial instruments (MiFID 2); Regulation (EU) 600/2014 of the European Parliament and the Council of 15 May 2014 on markets in financial instruments (MiFIR 2); Regulation (EU) 2017/1129 of the European Parliament and the Council of 14 June 2017 on the prospectus to be published when securities are offered to the public or admitted to trading on a regulated market (Prospectus Regulation); Regulation (EU) 596/2014 of the European Parliament and the Council of 16 April 2014 on market abuse (MAR); Directive 2014/57/EU of the European Parliament and the Council of 16 April 2014 on criminal sanctions for market abuse (MAD).

4 Directive 2009/110/EC of the European Parliament and of the Council of 16 September 2009, on the taking up, pursuit and prudential supervision of the business of electronic money institutions (EMD).

5 MiCA Regulation, Art. 3(1)(5).

case, the legislator favours the criterion of form over substance. Why? Because the form – the technology used – is, in fact, the only thing that all crypto-assets have in common, despite their differences in substance. Therefore, a crypto-asset is an asset based on cryptographic technology and registered on a blockchain.

§ 2. A PRINCIPLE OF TECHNOLOGICAL NEUTRALITY

7. The second methodological element introduced by the European lawmaker lies in the recognition that, although the technological criterion is a determining element, it is not absolute. Indeed, the legislator very clearly upholds a principle of technological neutrality.[6] Ultimately, it does not matter whether the asset is encrypted, or how it is represented: the nature of the asset depends on its substance, not its form. Consequently, the mere fact that an asset is registered on a blockchain is insufficient to alter its inherent nature. The MiCA Regulation reaffirms the principle of functional equivalence, which translates as 'same activities, same risks, same rules'.[7] If a crypto-asset is a currency in reality, it will have the nature of a currency; it is the case of Central Bank Digital Currency (CBDC), which is issued and/or guaranteed by a Central Bank as an official currency. Likewise, if a crypto-asset is a financial instrument in reality, it will have the nature of a financial instrument. This principle of technological neutrality is essential to the definition of a crypto-asset. However, it also gives rise to significant challenges at the qualification stage, as it permits the overlapping of legal qualifications. A crypto-asset may, therefore, also qualify as a financial instrument or an e-money. Accordingly, the principle of technological neutrality gives precedence to the criterion of substance over that of form.

8. The European lawmaker has engaged in a delicate balancing exercise in this context. The principle of technological neutrality, which is based on indifference to the technological medium, would have justified a mere adaptation of existing texts in order to accommodate new technologies, thereby avoiding the need for autonomous legal instruments.[8] In this vein, the scope of the Markets in Financial Instruments Directive (MIF 2 Directive) could have been

---

6 On the limits of the principle of technological neutrality, see V. Gautrais, 'Neutralité technologique - Rédaction et interprétation des lois face aux changements technologiques', *Les Editions Thémis*, May 2012. *Adde*, C. Reed, 'Taking sides on technology neutrality', *SCRIPT-ed*, Vol. 4, Issue 3, September 2007, pp. 263–84; B.-J. Koops, 'Should ICT Regulation Be Technology-Neutral?' in B.-J. Koops, M. Lips, C. Prins and M. Schellekens (eds.), *Starting Points for ICT Regulation: Deconstructing Prevalent Policy One-Liners*, IT & Law Series, Vol. 9, The Hague, T.M.C. Asser Press, 2006, pp. 77–108.

7 MiCA Regulation, recital (9).

8 The principle of technological neutrality does not mean that new technologies have no impact on the application of existing laws, but that they must not be favoured or disadvantaged in relation to pre-existing technologies, and must be treated equally.

extended to cover these new crypto-assets.[9] However, with the MiCA Regulation, the European policymaker marks a departure from this approach, establishing a dedicated regulatory framework grounded in the principle of functional equivalence. The aim is to enable new service providers to access the market on fair terms, by introducing lighter access conditions than those imposed on traditional providers in the financial sector. At the same time, the EU legislator seeks to prevent these new actors from bypassing the mandatory regulatory architecture already in place for financial markets. This dual ambition raises complex issues concerning regulatory coherence and articulation.

§ 3. AN OPEN-ENDED TYPOLOGY OF CRYPTO-ASSETS

9. Finally, the third key element introduced by the MiCA Regulation concerns the typology of crypto-assets, as established in its autonomous legal framework. In this context, the legislator adopts an enumerative approach – a technique previously used to define financial instruments, for example – rather than relying on a substantive criterion.[10]

10. The regulation identifies three main categories of crypto-assets.[11] First, electronic money tokens or *e-money tokens* (EMTs), which are backed by fiat currency and operate on the e-money model. The MiCA Regulation qualifies these instruments as e-money, reasoning by assimilation. Second, *'asset-referenced tokens'* (ARTs), which refer to assets other than a single official currency (e.g. commodities, a basket of currencies, etc.). These two categories are referred to as stablecoins. Third, a residual or 'catch-all' category, designed to encompass all other types of tokens. As the MiCA Regulation explicitly points out, this last category 'encompasses a wide range of crypto-assets, including utility tokens'.[12] This final category, which is non-exhaustive and is intended to capture any future innovations, poses the greatest difficulty in terms of articulation with the category of financial instruments.

11. In summary, the MiCA Regulation favours a technical definition of what constitutes a crypto-asset, coupled with the principle of technological neutrality.

---

9 See, e.g. Regulation (EU) 2022/858 of the European Parliament and of the Council of 30 May 2022 on a pilot scheme for market infrastructures based on distributed ledger technology, which amends the definition of financial instruments set out in Article 4(1)(15) of MiFID II, which now reads: '"Financial instruments" means the instruments referred to in Section C of Annex I, *including where such instruments are issued using distributed ledger technology*.'

10 F. Drummond, *Droit financier*, Economica, 2020, no. 261 *et seq.*; T. Bonneau, P. Pailler, A.-C. Rouaud, R. Vabres and A. Tehrani, *Droit financier*, 5th ed., LGDJ/Lextenso, Paris, 2025, spec. no. 769 *et seq.*

11 MiCA Regulation, recital 18.

12 MiCA Regulation, recital 18. *Adde*, Art. 3(1)(9): '"utility token": a type of crypto-asset intended solely to give access to a good or service provided by its issuer'.

It deliberately rejects any substantive definition in favour of an open-ended list – since utility tokens are just one example of the latest subcategory of tokens – which could incorporate new assets in the future. Nonetheless, the practical application of this method poses some difficulties.

SECTION II. THE IMPLEMENTATION OF THE METHOD

12. While the EU's preference for substance over form appears conceptually sound, its practical implementation has proven to be challenging. Two key examples illustrate these difficulties. The first relates to the qualification of a crypto-asset as a financial instrument (1). If a crypto-asset confers the same rights as a financial instrument, it should qualify accordingly as a financial instrument and fall under the regulatory framework governing financial markets. However, a major obstacle lies in the lack of a clear and comprehensive definition of 'financial instrument' under European law, which makes the distinction between financial instruments and crypto-assets particularly complex. The second example concerns e-money tokens, which qualify as e-money under the MiCA regulation (2). This qualification raises specific questions regarding the interplay between the MiCA Regulation, the E-money Directive,[13] and the Payment Services Directive.[14]

§ 1. THE ARTICULATION OF THE CONCEPTS OF 'CRYPTO-ASSET' AND 'FINANCIAL INSTRUMENT'

13. In some cases, the crypto-asset is undoubtedly a financial instrument. This applies, of course, to financial securities that have been 'tokenised'; in other words, conventional financial securities issued by a conventional company that are not registered in a securities account, but on a blockchain. This option is available in some Member States, such as France,[15] and is authorised even for

---

13 Directive 2009/110/EC of the European Parliament and of the Council of 16 September 2009, on the taking up, pursuit and prudential supervision of the business of electronic money institutions (EMD).

14 Directive (EU) 2015/2366 of the European Parliament and of the Council of 25 November 2015, on payment services in the internal market (PSD 2).

15 Since ordinance no. 2017-1674 of 8 December 2017, supplemented by decree no. 2018-1226 of 24 December 2018, art. L211-7 of the French Monetary Code provides for the possibility, for an issuer, of issuing unlisted financial securities and registering them on a blockchain. In Article L. 211-3, para. 2 of the Monetary and Financial Code, the legislator provides in this case for a principle of equivalence of registrations in a securities account and in a blockchain. The solution was extended to financial securities admitted to trading on 'DLT market infrastructure' by Law no. 2023-171 of 9 March 2023, in application of the pilot Regime Regulation.

listed financial securities, provided they are admitted to trading on a 'DLT market infrastructure' under the Pilot Regime Regulation.[16] In this case, they are traditional financial securities within the meaning of the MIF 2 Directive: if the medium changes (blockchain instead of a securities account), which may give rise to specific uncertainties,[17] they are regarded as financial securities. They therefore undoubtedly fall within the scope of financial market regulations.

14. Broadly speaking, all security tokens may be considered as 'tokenised' financial securities. Security tokens are not formally financial securities, but they are digital tokens that contractually replicate the financial rights (e.g. dividend entitlement) or even the political rights of a financial security. These rights are determined by the token issuance contract and can sometimes be integrated into a smart contract, in particular to ensure the payment of financial flows to token holders, or to enable them to exercise governance prerogatives via voting rights. While not formally securities, these pure digital tokens operate on the same model as financial securities via a blockchain. On the basis of the principle of technological neutrality, they too should be included in the category of financial securities and be subject to the MIF 2 Directive. The same applies to structured debt securities that entitle the holder to a payout based on the performance of an underlying asset (for example, exchange-traded commodities or exchange-traded funds). Such security tokens could also be classified as units or shares in collective investment schemes, or as derivatives.

15. However, there are some uncertainties, and we may ask whether the crypto-asset should be qualified as a financial instrument. In order to provide a clear and definitive answer as to when a crypto-asset should ultimately be classified as a financial instrument, the latter would have to meet clear and substantial criteria. However, this is not the case. Neither the notion of a financial instrument as set out in the MIF 2 Directive nor the notion of a crypto-asset as set out in the MiCA Regulation specifies any substantive criteria.[18] Once again, the European policymaker has adopted an enumerative approach, seeking to

---

16 For conditions, see Regulation (EU) 2022/858 of the European Parliament and of the Council of 30 May 2022 on a pilot scheme for market infrastructures based on distributed ledger technology, Art. 3. *Adde*, F. Gilbert, 'Régime pilote et nouveaux entrants', *BJB* 2023, no.201e4, p. 55; M. Lucchesi and B. Raisse, 'Le règlement européen sur le régime pilote: l'innovation réglementaire pour les infrastructures de marché en blockchain face au défi de sa mise en œuvre', RDBF 2022, Etude 10; C. Saudo, '*Régime Pilote* regulation: market infrastructure authorised to test distributed ledger technologies', *La Revue des Juristes de Science Po*, 2023, p. 16; S. Cabossioras and J. Nivot, 'Le futur règlement européen instaurant un régime pilote pour les infrastructures de marché sur la blockchain', *BJB* 2022, no.200q0, p. 41.

17 V. Malassigné, 'Le principe d'équivalence de l'inscription en compte et de l'inscription dans un dispositif d'enregistrement partagé" in, V. Magnier and P. Barban (dir.), *Blockchain et droit des sociétés* Thèmes et commentaires, Paris, Dalloz, 2019, p. 37.

18 See M. Lehmann and F. Schinerl, 'The Concept of Financial Instruments: Drawing the Borderline between MiFID and MiCAR', *EBI Working Paper Series*, 2024, no. 171.

retain the broadest possible definition, in order to incorporate new assets as they emerge. In the MIF 2 Directive, the list covers eleven points, some of which are redundant – seven of these concern derivatives, with some overlaps. Therefore, the list does not correspond to one or more identified criterion or criteria and covers both transferable securities and derivatives. For derivatives, for example, the Directive states that all instruments equivalent to the enumerated derivatives are included in the category of financial instruments. Furthermore, in addition to traditional financial instruments such as securities and derivatives, the category also includes greenhouse gas emission allowances; these are not financial instruments per se, but the EU policymaker wanted to control the risk of fraud with them. The definition of financial instruments is functional and deliberately flexible; when defining the scope of the financial regulatory framework, the European policymaker has adopted an assimilative approach.

16. In light of the legislator's uncertainty in this regard, the MiCA Regulation refers to guidelines from the European Securities and Markets Authority (ESMA) to determine the distinction between financial instruments and crypto-assets. In the absence of clear qualifying criteria, ESMA can only propose a set of indicators to identify converging practices that could enable certain crypto-assets to be classified as financial instruments. However, the Authority emphasises that this analysis must ultimately be conducted on a case-by-case basis, taking into account the specific nature of the rights conferred, which introduces legal uncertainty to the sector.[19] These difficulties relating to the classification of financial instruments are far from isolated. The same problem arises with regard to the classification of deposits and insurance contracts. The European supervisory authorities have, therefore, published joint guidelines setting out a standardised test for classifying assets.[20] In these guidelines, they emphasise once again that the regulatory classification of a crypto-asset must be carried out on a case-by-case basis, taking into account the applicable European and national law, the decisions of the Court of Justice of the EU, the decisions of national courts, and any regulatory measures or guidance applicable at national level.

§ 2. THE ARTICULATION OF THE CONCEPTS OF 'E-MONEY TOKENS', 'E-MONEY', AND 'FUNDS'

17. A second example concerns e-money tokens and their interplay with the pre-existing categories set out in the E-Money Directive and in the Payment Services Directive. Based on the principle of technological neutrality, the MiCA

---

19 ESMA, 'Guidelines on the conditions and criteria for the qualification of crypto-assets as financial instruments', 17 December 2024.

20 ESAs, 'Guidelines on templates for explanations and opinions, and the standardised test for the classification of crypto-assets', 10 December 2024.

Regulation deems e-money tokens to be e-money.[21] This means they are subject to the E-Money Directive. However, as the issuance of electronic money tokens exposes the issuer to specific risks that electronic money does not, the issuer must comply with certain additional obligations set out in the MiCA Regulation. Therefore, e-money token service providers are subject to the cumulative application of the texts. In this case, the principle of technological neutrality is, paradoxically, weakened, since technological specificity implies compliance with additional rules.

18. Moreover, the categorisation of electronic money as 'funds' within the meaning of Payment Services Directive 2 (PSD2)[22] raises certain questions about the applicable regime. Notably, it is unclear which regime applies to the transfer of e-money tokens, as these could potentially be subject to both the crypto-asset transfer service regulated by the MiCA Regulation and the funds transfer regime of the PSD2. This would mean that the service provider would have to comply with two sets of rules – those for crypto-asset service providers and those for payment service providers – and obtain dual authorisation, which seems disproportionate. The European Banking Authority (EBA) issued an Opinion on the interplay between PSD2 and the MiCA Regulation with regard to crypto-asset service providers that transact e-money tokens.[23] This Opinion was issued in response to a written request from the EU Commission dated 6 December 2024, requesting the EBA, in close cooperation with ESMA, to clarify the interplay. In this Opinion, which takes the form of a no-action letter, the EBA attempts to find a compromise. It specifies that the exchange of crypto-assets for funds and the exchange of crypto-assets for other crypto-assets are not considered payment services. However, it considers the transfer of crypto-assets involving electronic money tokens on behalf of customers, as well as the custody and administration of electronic money tokens, to be payment services. Furthermore, it states that custodial wallets holding electronic money tokens on behalf of one or more clients, which enable the transfer of tokens, should be classified as payment accounts. In this context, the European Authority advises national authorities to subject entities to a simplified procedure, or even grant them an exemption from authorisation as payment service providers until 1 March 2026, and, when they obtain authorisation, to deprioritise certain obligations. This uncertain regulatory framework highlights the limitations of the MiCA Regulation.

---

21 MiCA Regulation, Art. 48(2): 'E-money tokens shall be deemed to be electronic money.'

22 PSD 2, Art. 4(25). See also Proposal for a Directive of the European Parliament and of the Council on payment services and electronic money services in the internal market of 28 June 2023, COM(2023), 366 final, recital (16): 'Regulation (EU) 2023/1114 of 31 May 2023 lays down that electronic money tokens shall be deemed to be electronic money. Electronic money tokens should therefore be included, as electronic money, in the definition of funds.'

23 EBA, Opinion on the interplay between PSD2 and MiCA in relation to crypto-asset service providers that transact electronic money tokens, EBA/Op/2025/08, 10 June 2025.

19. In conclusion, these considerations highlight the complexity of designing an effective and proportionate regulatory framework for crypto-assets. A case-by-case analysis seems to prevail, although it does not necessarily guarantee certainty for the sector.

CHAPTER 2

TAXONOMY OF DIGITAL ASSETS IN THE EMIRATES: THE FSRA MODEL

By Edmond O'Hanlon[1] on 20 February 2025, Symposium *'Regulation of crypto-assets - Comparative law United Arab Emirates / European Union'* at Sorbonne University Abu Dhabi.

SECTION I. OPENING REMARKS

1. It is my pleasure to present to you the Abu Dhabi Global Market's (ADGM's) approach to regulating 'crypto', which we call 'Virtual Assets' (VA). As we are focused on taxonomy, we will cover the definitions of VA and stablecoins, which we call 'Fiat-Referenced Tokens' (FRTs).

SECTION II. BACKGROUND ON ADGM AND FSRA

2. Before we look at the definitions of VAs and FRTs, let me first please explain to you that the ADGM is a metaphorical common law island (on the actual Al Maryah and Reem Islands in Abu Dhabi) located in the civil law ocean that is the rest of the United Arab Emirates. The ADGM is an 'International Financial Centre'[2] and 'Financial Free Zone' which has been operating since October 2015.

3. Abu Dhabi Law No. (4) of 2013 established the ADGM, comprising of the Financial Services Regulatory Authority (FSRA), the Registration Authority (a corporate and commercial registrar), and the ADGM Courts. Under Federal Law No. 8 of 2004 on Financial Free Zones, like other Financial Free Zones in the United Arab Emirates, ADGM is subject to UAE Federal AML law[3] and:

> all provisions of Federal law <u>with the exception of the Federal civil and commercial laws</u>. [underline added]

---

1 Legal Counsel, Financial Services Regulatory Authority, Abu Dhabi Global Market. All views expressed are the author's views only and do not reflect those of the FSRA, ADGM, or its staff. The FSRA's framework was amended in June 2025.

2 See https://waifc.finance/ko/opinions/why-do-financial-centers-matter/.

3 Federal Decree Law No. 20 of 2018, as amended by Federal Decree Law No. 26 of 2021 and Federal Decree Law No. 7 of 2024. See https://uaelegislation.gov.ae/en/legislations/1016.

4. Pursuant to an ADGM law called the Application of English Law Regulations 2015,[4] the common law of England (including its rules of equity) applies in the ADGM, subject to:

(i) modifications that the ADGM believes are necessary; and

(ii) any amendments made to the common law of England by an ADGM law.

English statutes will not apply automatically in ADGM unless and until an ADGM law expressly adopts such English statute (or part of it) as having legal effect in the ADGM. This direct application of English law, and the adaptability and legal certainty that that brings, has allowed the ADGM to attract financial services firms.

5. The FSRA is responsible for authorising and supervising financial services activities carried out within ADGM, the International Financial Centre of Abu Dhabi. As a member of the International Organization of Securities Commissions (IOSCO), the FSRA has a robust regulatory framework that is aligned with international best practices developed by international standard-setting bodies, including IOSCO, and continuously seeks to improve it in line with global regulatory developments.

SECTION III. BACKGROUND ON FSRA VA REGULATION

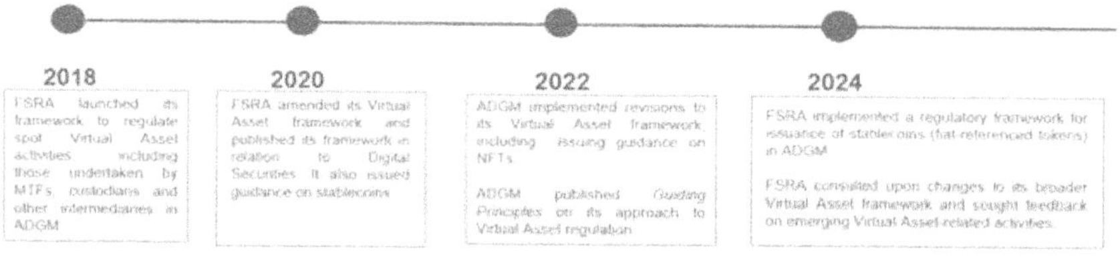

6. It is worth recapping that the FSRA pioneered a comprehensive regulatory framework for spot[5] trading in VAs back in June 2018. By comprehensive, I mean a full suite of regulatory requirements to offer regulated financial services in respect of VAs and not just a basic AML registration, including consumer protection, technology governance, client asset safekeeping, investor disclosure,

---

[4] See https://en.adgm.thomsonreuters.com/sites/default/files/net_file_store/ADGM1547_14585_VER2022.pdf.

[5] Derivatives trading in VA is covered as a Specified Investment. See p. 5 of FSRA's VA Guidance, defined ahead.

and requirements for intermediaries such as custodians, brokers, and Multilateral Trading Facilities.[6]

7. A key feature of the FSRA's model was the adoption of an Accepted Virtual Asset (AVA) regime.[7] Under the AVA regime, certain financial services called 'Regulated Activities' (set out in the FSRA's principal legalisation)[8] may only be conducted within ADGM where both the specific VA (i.e. the so-called 'asset-level' assessment), as well as the relevant firm's systems and controls (i.e. the so-called 'firm-level' assessment), have been assessed as satisfactory by the FSRA on a case-by-case basis. Given the nascent adoption of VA as a form of investment, as well as the potential use of VA to circumvent anti-money laundering measures, at the time the FSRA believed it prudent to adopt a cautious approach to the use of VA in ADGM.

8. Back in 2018, the FSRA took a pioneering position in deciding that VAs were different from securities and should be treated and regulated *like* commodities. In 2020 we published a framework on 'Digital Securities'[9] to distinguish Digital Securities from VAs, and we had separate guidance on stablecoins. In 2022 we issued guidance on how non-fungible tokens (NFTs) can be used in ADGM.

9. In 2020, the framework evolved from one that categorised all VA businesses within one Regulated Activity, '*Operating a Crypto-Asset Business*',[10] to a more sophisticated model that authorised firms to conduct specific Regulated Activities in relation to VA. Existing VA-specific rules and the FSRA's practice of considering the use of each additional VA on a firm-by-firm basis remained unchanged, consistent with developing best practice and international standards at the time.

---

6 A trading venue and alternative to a traditional stock exchange. MTFs facilitate the exchange of financial instruments between multiple parties, and are a 'multilateral system' in the sense that they allow multiple third-party buying and selling of financial instruments in a non-discretionary manner.

7 Para. 24 of the FSRA's VA Guidance, defined ahead.

8 See the Financial Services and Markets Regulations 2015 (FSMR): https://en.adgm.thomsonreuters.com/sites/default/files/net_file_store/ADGM1547_12483_VER26020125.pdf.

9 See FSRA, 'Guidance – Regulation of Digital Securities Activities in ADGM' (24 February 2020) at https://assets.adgm.com/download/assets/guidance-on-regulation-of-digital-securities-activities-in-adgm.pdf/f57b23cc3a0a11ef857b6e984d6ae48f?la=en&hash=EDCDD88518578D9E914BC2A27879755F, which states that: 'For the purposes of this Guidance, 'Digital Securities' are defined are types of digital assets that possess the features and characteristics of a Security (as defined in Schedule 1 – Part 3 of Specified Investments of FSMR). 4 Digital Securities also include 'tokenised' offerings of Securities.' and 'If a digital/virtual token being offered is assessed to exhibit the (economic and legal) features and characteristics of a Security, the FSRA will deem the digital/virtual token (being a 'Digital Security') as a Security pursuant to Section 58(2)(b) of FSMR.'

10 See Consultation Paper No. 2 of 2018 – Introduction of Crypto Asset Regulatory Framework in ADGM: 608b373a7fc311ef9f55063684d039e9.

10. Despite some choppy waters in the VA sector over the past few years, the ADGM has retained its reputation for prudent and proportionate VA regulation. As a member of IOSCO, the FSRA has a robust regulatory framework that is aligned with international best practices. IOSCO produced detailed Policy Recommendations for Crypto and Digital Asset Markets in November 2023,[11] and I am glad to say that the FSRA has already been implementing similar policies for a number of years.

11. It is fair to say that the FSRA has taken a careful and considered approach to the use of VAs within the ADGM, and that will continue to be the case. Out of the universe of VAs,[12] currently the FSRA has approved a total of 80 AVAs and 4 stablecoins or fiat tokens (on 12 networks), per the FSRA's VA Guidance – see the following page.

11 See https://www.iosco.org/library/pubdocs/pdf/IOSCOPD747.pdf.

12 Estimates vary widely, but for the sake of argument let us say that it is more than 20,000 in total, with the world's biggest crypto exchange having more than 500 VAs.

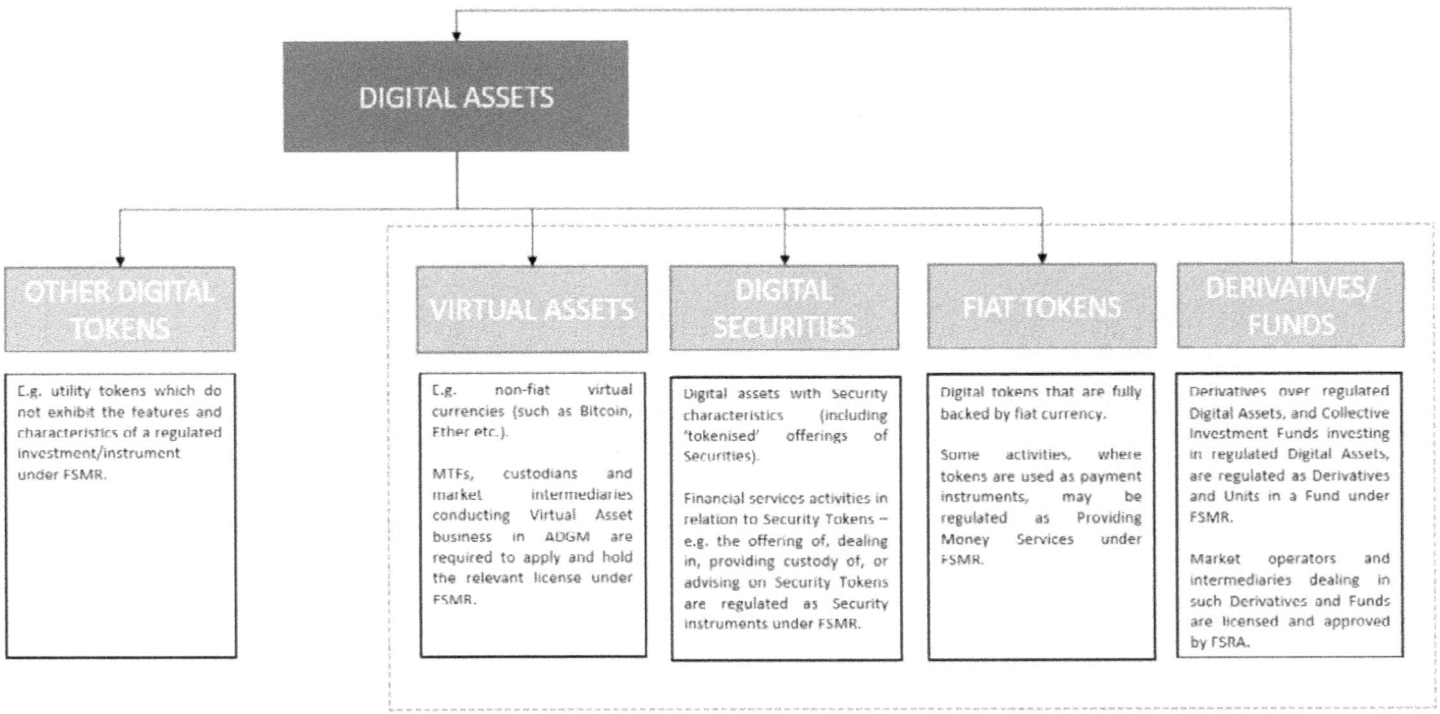

The FSRA regulates, and will allow to operate within the ADGM, the Digital Assets located within the blue dotted line and Derivatives over/Funds investing in Digital Assets.

12. This diagram neatly depicts the FSRA's thinking on digital assets and you can see that we have clarified the conceptual distinctions between 'Digital Securities' (i.e. traditional financial instruments that are tokenised) from VAs, and from other digital tokens which are not VAs.

§ 1. DIGITAL ASSETS

13. The largest bucket within which everything fits is a digital asset. We do not have an actual definition for the term 'digital asset', but even if we did, it would likely be so broad as to only have limited practical use, because a digital asset could be anything in digital form. The UK Law Commission's definition of 'digital asset' shows how broad a concept it is,[8] as does the Unidroit definition (i.e. an electronic record which is capable of being controlled).[14]

§ 2. VIRTUAL ASSETS

14. Within that very broad understanding of digital assets, the FSRA has subdivided VAs from everything else. It is possible to obtain a licence from the FSRA to offer certain Regulated Activities (i.e. financial services in FSMR) in respect of a VA, but only if the FSRA assesses that it is an Accepted Virtual Asset (AVA), which I will come to later.

§ 3. OTHER DIGITAL TOKENS

15. For cryptos that are not AVAs, such as pure utility tokens, it may be possible to seek registration under the Registration Authority's DLT Foundation Regulation,[15] which gives distributed autonomous organisations a 'legal wrapper' when interacting with parties off-chain in the real or non-blockchain world. Introduced in November 2023, there are already eight registered DLT Foundations.

---

8 See https://lawcom.gov.uk/project/digital-assets/: "Any asset that is represented digitally or electronically. There are many different types of digital assets, not all of which will be capable of being things to which personal property rights can relate. In this report, we use the term in a broad sense."

14 See Unidroit Principles on Digital Assets and Private Law, at https://www.unidroit.org/wp-content/uploads/2024/01/Principles-on-Digital-Assets-and-Private-Law-linked-1.pdf.

15 See https://en.adgm.thomsonreuters.com/sites/default/files/net_file_store/ADGM1547_26199_VER94959.pdf.

§ 4. DIGITAL SECURITIES

16. Digital Securities[16] are merely tokenised securities and the FSRA's framework for securities applies equally to Digital Securities. An instrument that does not quite neatly fit within the definition of a security in our legislation, but which should nonetheless be regarded as a security, can be deemed by the FSRA to be a security under FSMR. So basically, financial services in relation to Digital Securities, such as their custody, dealing, and advising, and operating primary or secondary markets, are subject to the normal regulatory requirements in FSMR that would apply to normal securities, which includes that intermediaries be licensed.

§ 5. DERIVATIVES ON VAS AND PARTICIPATION BY COLLECTIVE INVESTMENT FUNDS IN VAS

17. Derivatives in VAs are regulated as Commodity Derivatives under FSMR[17] within the wider definition of 'Specified Investments' covering all of FSMR's investment classes except VAs.[18] A Collective Investment Fund (per FSMR) investing in VAs issues Units, which are another form of 'Specified Investment'.

§ 6. FIAT TOKENS

18. These are stablecoins which the FSRA calls 'Fiat-Referenced Tokens' (FRTs). It is interesting to note that we do not regard stablecoins to be VAs; essentially that is because we regard VAs as being 'like' commodities and, as we know, the price of commodities fluctuates, while the value of a stablecoin should not.

---

16 Defined on p. 5 of the FSRA's 'Guidance on Regulation of Virtual Asset Activities in ADGM' (2 January 2025) (FSRA's VA Guidance), at https://en.adgm.thomsonreuters.com/sites/default/files/net_file_store/Guidance_-_Virtual_Asset_Activities_in_ADGM_(VER06.020125).pdf, to mean: '"Digital Securities" (e.g., digital/virtual tokens that have the features and characteristics of a Security under FSMR (such as Shares, Debentures and Units in a Collective Investment Fund)).'

17 Page 5 of the FSRA's VA Guidance read together with the definition of 'Commodity Derivative' in s. 258 of FSMR.

18 Sch. 1, pt. 3 of FSMR.

SECTION 4. FSRA DEFINITION OF 'VIRTUAL ASSET'

19. The FSRA's definition of a Virtual Asset is as follows:

*"**Virtual Asset**" means a digital representation of value that can be digitally traded and functions as (1) a medium of exchange; and/or (2) a unit of account; and/or (3) a store of value, but does not have legal tender status in any jurisdiction. A Virtual Asset is -*

(a) neither issued nor guaranteed by any jurisdiction, and fulfils the above functions only by agreement within the community of users of the Virtual Asset; and

(b) distinguished from Fiat Currency[6] and E-money[7]."

20. What can be derived from this definition is that a VA is:

1) in digital form/digitally native;
2) has some form of value;
3) is privately issued rather than issued by a public authority or with the approval of a public authority; and
4) does not have legal tender status anywhere.

21. Bitcoin was recognised as an AVA by the FSRA before El Salvador recognised it as legal tender in September 2021; now that Bitcoin is essentially no longer legal tender in El Salvador, it seems the FSRA's definition of VA was correct to exclude tokenised legal tender. It may seem obvious in retrospect, but recall that a lot of juridictions struggled with making these basic and essential clarifications for years, so it was quite innovative for the FSRA to have done so in 2018.

22. In time, the FSRA's VA definition may need to be updated to exclude Central Bank Digitial Currencies (CBDCs). Note that the reference to 'e-money' is not the same as it is understood in EU law. For FSRA purposes, e-money means tokenised bank deposits, which are likewise excluded from the definiton of VAs.

23. Note the lack of an *explicit* reference to blockchain or distributed ledger technologies (DLT) in the definition of VA. It is implied that a VA will operate on a DLT in the other parts of the FSRA's VA Guidance, but as there are many different types of architecture in designing DLT (from highly decentralised and permissionless, to highly centralised and permissioned, and some which are not strictly blockchain-based), it was felt that it was not necessary to make this a central component of the definiton of a VA.

24. Interestingly, in the UK the Financial Services and Markets Act 2023 defines a crypto asset as something "which may include distributed ledger technology",[19] so this acknolwedges the need for a wide definition to cover a range of emerging technologies.

[19] S. 69(4) of FSMA 2023. Underline added. See https://www.legislation.gov.uk/ukpga/2023/29/section/69/enacted.

25. The key thing to remember with the FSRA's definition of a VA is that VAs, per the FSRA's VA Guidance are:

> Treated as commodities and, therefore, not deemed Specified Investments under FSMR.[20]

26. This is not to say that VAs are *actually* commodities like oil or gold; rather, it is saying that they behave like commodities (i.e. their value fluctuates up and down depending on supply and demand features).

SECTION V. OUTSIDE THE DEFINITION OF 'VIRTUAL ASSET'

§ 1. DIGITAL SECURITIES

27. As you know, securities (in the common law) are a legal or property interest in a common venture such as a company, and their value is dependent on the success or failure of that venture. For VAs, while the English common law recognises them as a form of property (or *"third category thing"* per the UK Law Commission's research),[21] they do not give their holder a legal or property interest in the issuer of the token.[22] In fact, given the technology of the blockchain and the development communities that support various blockchains, they can even survive the collapse of their issuer, unlike securities. Consequently, this is what distinguishes VAs from securities.

28. However, if the FSRA examines a particular project that calls itself a VA, and we find that it gives a legal interest in the issuer of the token, then we would regard it as sufficiently like a security that we would deem it to be a security under section 58(2)(b) FSMR and, what's more, treat it as a Digital Security so that the FSRA's regular securities rules, and the FSRA's Digital Securities Guidance[23] will apply to the tokenisation elements.

---

20 See the FSRA's VA Guidance. Underline added.

21 See https://webarchive.nationalarchives.gov.uk/ukgwa/20250109172211mp_/https://s3-eu-west-2.amazonaws.com/cloud-platform-e218f50a4812967ba1215eaecede923f/uploads/sites/30/2023/06/Final-digital-assets-report-FOR-WEBSITE-2.pdf.

22 Cryptocurrencies such as Bitcoin or Tether (USDT) can attract property rights under English law. This is a new, distinct form of property right, not premised on an underlying legal right. It is neither a chose in action nor a chose in possession. See *Tulip Trading v. Bitcoin* [2024] EWCA Civ 83; *D'Aloia v. Persons Unknown* [2024] EWHC 2342 (Ch); and the UK Property (Digital Assets Etc.) Bill, at https://www.gov.uk/government/publications/property-digital-assets-etc-bill/property-digital-assets-etc-bill-factsheet.

23 See FSRA, 'Guidance – Regulation of Digital Securities Activities in ADGM' (24 February 2020), at https://assets.adgm.com/download/assets/guidance-on-regulation-of-digital-securities-activities-in-adgm.pdf/f57b23cc3a0a11ef857b6e984d6ae48f?la=en&hash=EDCDD88518578D9E914BC2A27879755F.

§ 2. ICOS

29. Initial coin offerings (ICOs), or anything that is intended for 'capital formation/capital raising purposes', are excluded from the definition of a VA per the FSRA's VA Guidance.

§ 3. NFTS

30. Unlike VAs, NFTs cannot be replicated, and thus cannot be traded or exchanged at equivalency. Essentially, therefore, NFTs operate similarly to a collector's item, but are digital instead of physical. Some NFT activities are allowed within ADGM, e.g. firms conducting own account or proprietary investments in NFTs are allowed to do so within ADGM, but that does not make them VAs.

§ 4. UTILITY TOKENS

31. Basically, 'pure' Utility Tokens (i.e. those that are used exclusively within their issuer's network and not more widely, and without any characteristic of an investment, or secondary trading) are not VAs, and are thus not capable of being AVAs. The FSRA's VA Guidance states that a Utilty Token is one which can be redeemed for access to a specific product or service, typically provided using a DLT platform, and does not exhibit the features and characteristics of a regulated investment/instrument under FSMR.

32. While the FSRA's VA Guidance is silent on the FSRA's policy stance, what it should say but doesn't is that the Utility Token can be redeemed by the issuer or from the issuer's group; if it is accepted more widely than that then it will cease to be a Utility Token even if it is described as such.

33. Recall that crypto 'exchange tokens' (while they may be described as 'utility tokens') will be VAs as they are 'hybrid' tokens available from networks not controlled by the issuer or the issuer's group of companies. The FSRA applies a substance-overform approach to Utility Tokens so, even if a token is marketed as, or commonly thought of as, a 'utility token', it can still be regarded as a VA by the FSRA as it has both utility and other characteristics, e.g. Binance Coin or BNB, also Basic Attention Token (available from the Brave web browser company), and Huobi Token are examples of hybrid tokens and are thus VAs, and have additionally been recognised by the FSRA as AVAs.

§ 5. FIAT-REFERENCED TOKENS

34. As mentioned, the FSRA distinguishes stablecoins, which are not supposed to fluctuate in value, from VAs, whose value can and does fluctuate in accordance with market demand.

SECTION VI. 'ACCEPTED VIRTUAL ASSETS'

§ 1. ONLY 'ACCEPTED VIRTUAL ASSETS' (AVAS) FOR CERTAIN REGULATED ACTIVITIES

35. As mentioned in the FSRA's VA Guidance, the FSRA has a general power and wide discretion to determine each AVA that will be permitted in relation to VA activities within ADGM in order to prevent potential higher-risk activities relating to illiquid or 'immature' VAs. While it imposes requirements on entities offering financial services in respect of VAs, and operates an AVA regime, it is important to note that the FSRA does not take a view on the merits of transacting or investing in VAs and neither endorses nor recommends them.

36. So what does *'accepted'* mean? It means that a VA passes the FSRA's assessment criteria so that certain financial services can be offered in respect of the VA in the ADGM.

§ 2. FSRA'S 7 ASSESSMENT CRITERIA FOR 'ACCEPTED VIRTUAL ASSETS'

37. Our current approach is that, for certain Regulated Activities in FSMR (listed below) which include a reference to 'Virtual Assets', an Authorised Person *must only* use AVAs for which the firm has received the prior approval of the FSRA before offering them to clients. AVAs are those VAs that the FSRA assesses as meeting the seven key factors outlined in Chapter 17 of the FSRA's Conduct of Business Rulebook[24] (COBS) and the FSRA VA Guidance.

38. FSRA approval can be broken down into two steps, one being the asset level for a particular VA itself, and the other being the firm level where the FSRA assesses an individual firm's proposed use of that VA. An important factor is the maturity or market capitalisation of a VA; the rationale for this is to screen out higher-risk and very 'immature' VAs. We also consider the security features of

---

[24] See the FSRA's 'Conduct of Business Rulebook' (COBS), at https://en.adgm.thomsonreuters.com/sites/default/files/net_file_store/ADGM1547_8841_VER17020125.pdf.

the VA and its ability to safeguard private keys, and, crucially, whether firms are able to demonstrate the origin and traceability of the users of the VA.

39. The seven factors are:

1) **Maturity:** and the controls and processes to manage volatility of a particular VA. There are no hard-and-fast rules or policies implemented regarding this factor or, indeed, any of the other factors, but until now it has typically been the case that a VA has not been recognised as an AVA until it has been issued and in circulation for several months.
   Recall that we do not entertain ICOs as VAs capable of being recognised as AVAs.
   This factor on maturity goes a considerable way towards reducing the extreme volatility of VAs involving abusive market practices of so-called 'rug pulls' or 'pump-and-dump schemes'.
2) **Security:** whether a specific VA is able to secure private keys per the requirements of Chapter 17 of COBS.
3) **Traceability/monitoring** (as mentioned, **this is a, or *the*, critical factor**): whether firms are able to demonstrate the origin and destination of the specific VA, if the VA enables the identification of counterparties to each transaction, and if on-chain transactions in the VA can be adequately monitored.
   Traceability is a fundamental criterion without which a VA will not be recognised as an AVA even if it has met all the other criteria. Privacy tokens will not be allowed.
4) **Exchange connectivity:** the number and jurisdiction of the exchanges supporting the VA and whether the FSRA considers that such exchanges are suitably regulated.
5) **Type of distributed ledger (DLT):** whether the VA leverages an existing DLT, or whether a new DLT has had its security and usability stress-tested.
6) **Innovation/efficiency:** whether the VA solves a fundamental problem; addresses an unmet market need.
7) **Practical application/function:** whether the VA has real-world, quantifiable, functionality. This criterion may be demonstrable, or it may be very subjective or even theoretical. It goes to help determine a VA from a pure utility token, which will not be a VA.

40. It is not really possible to demarcate these seven criteria between the asset-level and firm-level assessments, as a lot of them are relevant to both assessments. For example, a VA may pass the traceability criterion at the asset level but the particular firm that proposes to use it may not have sufficient systems and controls to satisfy the FSRA's traceability requirements, and so that VA will not be approved as an AVA for that particular firm.

41. It is, therefore, important to recall that the AVA assessment is *a firm-specific assessment*, and just because one firm can offer a Regulated Activity in respect of an AVA does not entitle a different firm to do so. Therefore, when a VA is recognised as an AVA, it is specific to that particular firm's offer of Regulated Activities. The list of AVAs does not entitle a different firm to offer any services in the AVA.

§ 3. CONSULTATION PAPER – REVIEW OF THE AVA PROCESS

42. To date, the FSRA has taken on the responsibility of assessing and approving or rejecting specific VAs submitted by firms for their use on a firm-by-firm basis, based on these seven key factors. After six years of operation, FSRA VA firms have gained a lot of experience operating in a regulated environment and their risk management and compliance systems have improved. Also, independent third-party tools such as Chainalysis, Elliptic, and many others have come to market, which significantly helps verify the traceability of VAs.

43. Therefore, at this juncture the FSRA considers it appropriate to consider permitting VA firms to play a more significant role in the assessment of VAs for use in the ADGM as AVAs for certain Regulated Activities. The FSRA proposal is to potentially allow firms to:

a) offer more VAs than currently is the case; and
b) expedite the time to market for such VAs, and facilitate the development of Web3.

44. In December 2024, the FSRA issued Consultation Paper No. 11 of 2024[25] to solicit public comment concerning revisions to the FSRA's VA regulatory framework, including the process for the recognition of AVAs. The Consultation Paper included proposals granting additional overarching regulatory powers to the FSRA to suspend VA transactions that contravened FSRA legislation or otherwise would not be in the interests of ADGM. The FSRA also proposed some fee, prudential, and capital related amendments, as well as changes to investment restrictions applicable to venture capital funds, enabling investment in VA issued by growth-phase companies.

45. A number of detailed responses were received from industry participants and their advisors, which, while supportive, suggested some amendments, in particular on our suggested changes to the AVA process. The FSRA is carefully considering those suggestions. Under proposals currently being considered, firms may have to:

1) devise their own VA assessment process using the seven key factors and other screening criteria developed by the FSRA;

---

[25] See Consultation_Paper_No._11_of_2024_-_Proposed_Amendments_to_theDigital_Asset_Regulatory_Framework.pdf.

2) give the FSRA prior notification of the firm's assessment; and
3) enable the FSRA to undertake follow-up spot checks on VAs the firm has approved.

§ 4. ONGOING ASSESSMENT AND FSRA FOLLOW-UP REVIEWS

46. *If* the FSRA permits firms to self-assess VAs, the FSRA will need to give careful consideration to how it would monitor such self-assessments. Self-assessment would not be a one-off exercise but would instead involve an initial assessment followed by an ongoing assessment. The precise requirements are being worked on currently.

§ 5. PROHIBITED TOKENS

47. 'Privacy Tokens' are not permissible in the FSRA's framework (e.g. a token which, *by design*, disguises or otherwise obfuscates, or purports to hide or obfuscate, details of its token holder or transaction history which would otherwise be visible to third parties through the DLT on which the token is hosted). It is not the case that a VA with privacy features will be automatically prohibited. What is automatically prohibited is a VA whose privacy features cannot be unwound or deselected, e.g. the so-called blinding features used by Monero, which also shield wallet amounts and their traceability by breaking transactions into many smaller amounts and mixing them up, making them nearly impossible to trace.

48. For example, there are two versions of Litecoin but only one of them (the one on the Litecoin network) can be an AVA, owing to the fact that the other one (on the MimbleWimble protocol) has features which cannot be deselected and which obscure the identity of the parties using it.

SECTION VII. FINANCIAL SERVICES AND MARKETS REGULATIONS (FSMR) – REGULATED ACTIVITIES

49. As mentioned, only AVAs can be used to provide certain RAs in the ADGM. Only certain financial services (i.e. Regulated Activities) refer to VAs. The following Regulated Activities can be undertaken in relation to VAs:

a) Dealing in Investments as Principal;
b) Dealing in Investments as Agent;
c) Advising on Investments or Credit;
d) Arranging Deals in Investments;
e) Managing Assets;

f) Providing Custody;
g) Arranging Custody; and
h) Operating a Multilateral Trading Facility (MTF).

50. Firms providing these Regulated Activities with AVAs are expected to satisfy the activity-specific conduct of business and prudential requirements which apply to such Regulated Activity generally, as well as the additional VA-specific requirements set out in Chapter 17 of COBS, which includes requirements on only using AVAs, technology governance requirements on wallets and keys, the travel rule on the origin and destination of the VAs, and additional rules on the disclosure of all material risks associated with VAs.

51. The FSRA's VA Guidance is the centrepiece of the FSRA's VA framework, containing our VA taxonomy and the seven assessment criteria that we apply to determining which VAs are AVAs. The FSRA's main goals for its VA framework include to provide:

1. a safe and sound market without unnecessary over-regulation; position ADGM as a destination of choice for legitimate virtual asset players;
2. a comprehensive, best-in-class framework with a high-water mark for the regulation of virtual asset activities, to effectively address the significant risks associated with these activities;
3. proper governance, oversight, and transparency over VA activities;
4. living and breathing guidance; and
5. a regime to attract conventional institutional players and large VA operators.

52. The FSRA operates according to six guiding principles the FSRA applies to its work with VAs:

1. A robust and transparent, risk-based regulatory framework
2. High standards for authorisation;
3. Preventing money laundering and other financial crime;
4. Risk-sensitive supervision;
5. Commitment to enforce on regulatory breaches; and
6. National and international cooperation.

53. The FSRA considers that there are five key risks in the VA space, as follows:

1. *AML/CTF/Tax*
   The FSRA AML Rulebook[26] applies in full to VA activities. Entities will need to comply with reporting obligations in relation to the US Foreign Account Tax Compliance Act (FATCA)[27] and Common Reporting Standard (CRS).[28]

---

26 See https://en.adgm.thomsonreuters.com/sites/default/files/net_file_store/ADGM1547_5692_VER09211223.pdf.

27 See https://www.irs.gov/businesses/corporations/foreign-account-tax-compliance-act-fatca.

28 See https://web-archive.oecd.org/tax/automatic-exchange/common-reporting-standard/standard-for-automatic-exchange-of-financial-account-information-in-tax-matters-second-edition-9789264267992-en.htm.

VA-tracing tools must be employed by VA firms, who are required to assess all deposits and withdrawals to detect the use of 'mixers' and 'tumblers'. While industry typically uses five wallet 'hops' to trace a transaction, the FSRA does not set a limit on the number of hops away from the last deposit into the VA firm's wallets in order to consider it properly traced. Firms should possess the capability of reviewing as many hops as the firm deems necessary. Firms should adopt a policy stance premised on a risk-based approach (as understood by the FSRA's AML Rulebook), to determine the basis for further scrutiny.

2. *Consumer Protection*
   All material risks associated with VAs generally, AVAs, and VA products, services, and activities must be disclosed.
3. *Technology Governance*
   Systems and controls must be in place in relation to VA wallets, origin and destination of VA funds, private keys, and security and risk management. This was included in our discussion of the seven key factors, and note that the IT Risk Management Guidance will shortly be converted to rules in the General Rulebook and COBS.
4. *Exchange-type Activities*
   VA trading platforms require market surveillance, settlement processes, transaction recording, transparency and public disclosure mechanisms, and exchange-like operational systems and controls.
5. *Custody*
   VA Custodians are regulated similarly to FSRA-regulated 'conventional' custodians. FSMR includes VA as within the meaning of 'Client Assets' and 'Client Investments',[29] but the FSRA requires more frequent reconciliations and reporting than for other Investments. The protection of VAs as Client Assets is a key consideration for the FSRA. The FSRA will not allow commingling. Client Assets are to be segregated and ring-fenced from the VA firm's own assets. Significantly, the FSRA will not allow rehypothecation of VAs. VA firms are not allowed to use Client Assets for their own purpose, including placing them as collateral with any other counterparties, e.g. for staking/borrowing/lending purposes.
   The FSRA requires weekly reconciliation and reporting of Client Assets held by VA Custodians.[30] This is more extensive than the best practices in traditional finance. A full list of Client Account cash book balances is required every five days, per COBS Rule 14.11.2.

[29] Per COBs para. 17.1.3 and the definition of Client Assets in the FSRA's Glossary (GLO).
[30] COBs, para. 17.8.4.

Post-speech

1. Following the speech on 20 February 2025, the FSRA's framework was amended in June 2025 in light of the feedback to the FSRA's Consultation Paper No. 11 of 2024.[31] The FSRA considers that the VA sector has matured considerably since the introduction of its framework in 2018, and VA assessment tools have grown in sophistication. The FSRA concluded that it is now an appropriate time for VA firms to be primarily responsible for assessing the VAs they propose to offer in conjunction with VA Regulated Activities. Accordingly, the FSRA has amended the VA assessment and approval process such that the FSRA's approval of each use as an AVA is no longer required. This development should expedite the time to market for VA firms in ADGM.[32]

2. The amendments to the VA assessment process:

a. impose an obligation upon each VA firm to conduct detailed due diligence per the criteria specified in COBS in respect of each VA it wishes to provide VA Regulated Activities in respect of;

b. require a VA firm to notify the FSRA using a prescribed form confirming the conduct of such due diligence at least five business days prior to deploying the proposed VA;

c. upon completion of the five-business-day period, permits the VA firm (in the absence of a communication from the FSRA) to consider the proposed VA as an AVA for that VA firm, and the VA firm may immediately commence the provision of certain Regulated Activities in respect of that AVA; and

d. enable the FSRA to exercise an additional VA-specific direction power in FSMR to impose restrictions or additional obligations, or to prohibit the use of such VA. This power will be available to the FSRA at all times, both during and after the five-business-day notification period.

3. Authorised Persons should note that an AVA previously accepted for use in the ADGM prior to June 2025 (i.e. accepted by the FSRA) shall retain its 'AVA' status for the Authorised Persons to whom it was granted, without that Authorised Person being required to assess and notify the FSRA of it. Importantly, however, such FSRA-approved AVA must be included on the Authorised Person's list of Accepted Virtual Assets published on its website, and is subject to the ongoing monitoring requirement outlined in COBS Rule 17.2.6.

4. Therefore, to avoid disruption to the recognition of existing AVAs, the FSRA has grandfathered the 107 AVAs from before June 2025 to the new regime by considering them 'accepted' for the purposes of the notification requirement placed on Authorised Persons in the new regime.

---

[31] See Consultation_Paper_No._11_of_2024_-_Proposed_Amendments_to_theDigital_Asset_Regulatory_Framework.pdf.

[32] See https://en.adgm.thomsonreuters.com/rulebook/10-june-fsra-rules-digital-assets.

5. The existing Guidance on Regulation of Virtual Asset Activities in ADGM (i.e. the FSRA's VA Guidance) has been reviewed and an updated version reflecting these changes was published alongside the proposed amendments in June 2025.[33] Additionally, the seven key factors of Chapter 17 of COBs have been amended to make certain clarifications.

6. The FSRA's long-standing policy stance of prohibiting 'privacy tokens' and 'algorithmic stablecoins' has been codified into FSMR.

7. The FSRA removed the Regulated Activity of Arranging Custody from the list of Regulated Activities to which the AVA requirement applies.

[33] See https://assets.adgm.com/download/assets/Guidance+Virtual+Asset+Activities+in+ADGM+20231218.pdf/f7702902704711efa4c3fe3e7821af93.

TITLE 2
THE REGULATION OF STABLECOINS

CHAPTER 1
STABLECOINS REGULATION IN THE EUROPEAN UNION

Hubert DE VAUPLANE*

SECTION I. EUROPEAN REGULATORY REGIME FOR STABLECOINS

§ 1. TYPOLOGY AND DEFINITIONS

1. Within the European Union (EU), stablecoins are governed by the MiCA Regulation,[1] which classifies them into two subcategories: e-money tokens (EMTs) and asset-referenced tokens (ARTs).

2. The MiCA Regulation defines ARTs as 'a type of crypto-asset that purports to maintain a stable value by referencing the value of one official currency'.[2] Conversely, EMTs are defined as 'a type of crypto-asset that is not an electronic money token and that purports to maintain a stable value by referencing another value or right or a combination thereof, including one or more official currencies'.[3] These two subcategories are subject to distinct legal regimes. The regime applicable to ARTs, which are considered to pose higher liquidity risks due to the volatility of the underlying assets, imposes stricter safeguards on issuers.

3. The regime imposed by the MiCA Regulation in relation to stablecoins is now in the process of being enforced across the entire EU. The MiCA Regulation has been enforceable since 1 January 2025, but for EMT and ART it entered into force on 30 June 2024.

* The author thanks Laetitia Kodjia for her help in drafting this chapter.

1 Regulation (EU) 2023/1114 of the European Parliament and of the Council of 31 May 2023 on markets in crypto-assets (MiCA Regulation).

2 Art. 3, MiCA Regulation.

3 ibid, Art. 3(6).

4. Indeed, in a public statement dated 17 January 2025, the European Securities and Markets Authority (ESMA) reminded European crypto-asset service providers (CASPs) that "as soon as possible and no later than the end of Q1 2025, CASPs offering certain crypto-asset services in the EU are expected to cease providing such services in relation to non-compliant ARTs or EMTs in the EU when their services constitute an offer to the public".[4]

§ 2. CONDITIONS OF AUTHORISATION AS A STABLECOIN ISSUER

5. The MiCA Regulation stipulates conditions for the authorisation of stablecoin issuers, which vary depending on the nature of the stablecoin issued.

6. With regard to the issuance of e-money tokens, in addition to the requirement that the issuing institution must be either a credit institution or an electronic money institution, issuers must also publish a crypto-asset White Paper and ensure that all commercial communications on their website are accurate. Issuers are liable for any incorrect information contained in the White Paper. Furthermore, they are required to establish both a recovery plan and a redemption plan to be implemented in the event that they are unable to meet their obligations to issue tokens at par upon receipt of funds, or to redeem tokens on demand and at par value.

7. As for issuers of asset-referenced tokens, these may be issued either by any legal person or undertaking established in the Union and authorised as an issuer of ARTs, or by an authorised credit institution. In both cases, the issuer must prepare a White Paper, which must be approved by the competent national authority[5] and published on the issuer's website. The issuer is also held liable for any inaccurate information contained therein.

§ 3. OBLIGATIONS OF STABLECOINS ISSUERS

8. The MiCA Regulation sets out clear obligations for issuers of stablecoins, according to whether the token qualifies as an asset-referenced token or an e-money token.

---

4 ESMA, 'Public Statement on the Provision of Certain Crypto-Asset Services in Relation to Non-MiCA Compliant ARTs and EMTs', 17 January 2025.

5 Art. 16(1), MiCA Regulation.

I. *Conduct and Governance Obligations*

9. Under the MiCA Regulation, the professional obligations imposed on issuers of asset-referenced tokens are further specified, given that such issuers are not, by default, regulated entities. In this regard, the MiCA Regulation provides that ART issuers must act honestly, fairly, and professionally; communicate with actual and potential holders of the tokens in a fair, clear, and non-misleading manner; act in the best interests of token holders and treat them equally; establish and maintain effective and transparent procedures for handling complaints promptly, fairly, and consistently; and identify, prevent, manage, and disclose any conflicts of interest.

10. Such obligations do not apply to issuers of EMTs, which are already subject to a prior authorisation requirement, either as credit institutions or as electronic money institutions, thereby offering a higher level of regulatory assurance to prospective token holders.

II. *Capital Requirements and Asset Reserves for Stablecoin Issuers*

11. In addition, the MiCA Regulation lays down detailed requirements regarding own funds and the reserve of assets applicable to stablecoin issuers. As regards ART issuers, they must maintain at all times a reserve of assets managed in such a way as to adequately cover the risks associated with the referenced assets and to address the liquidity risks arising from the permanent redemption rights of token holders. This reserve must be legally segregated from the issuer's own estate and excluded from the pool of assets subject to claims from the issuer's creditors.[6] ARTs issuers are also required to maintain own funds equal to at least the highest of the following: 350,000 euros; 2% of the average amount of the reserve assets; or one-quarter of the fixed overheads of the preceding financial year.[7]

12. By contrast, issuers of EMTs are already subject to distinct own funds requirements under sectoral legislation applicable to their status as regulated institutions, and are, therefore, not subject to additional own funds requirements under the MiCA Regulation. Nevertheless, they remain obliged to maintain a sufficiently liquid reserve, ensuring a 1:1 backing ratio (meaning that one e-money token pegged to the euro corresponds to one euro). MiCA allows such issuers to invest part of the funds received in exchange for EMTs in secure, low-risk assets, provided these qualify as highly liquid financial instruments with minimal market, credit, and concentration risk. In any case, and for issuers who are not credit institutions but electronic money institutions, at least 30% of the

---

6 ibid, Art. 36(2).

7 ibid, Art. 35(1).

funds received by issuers of EMTs must be held in segregated accounts with credit institutions.

III. Disclosure Obligations through the White Paper

13. The White Paper published by stablecoin issuers prior to issuance must contain comprehensive information intended to inform the public, including information about the issuer of the token, the characteristics of the token, the public offer, the underlying technology, the risks involved, and the rights and obligations attached to the token. In the specific case of ARTs, the White Paper must also include information relating to the reserve of assets.

14. From now on, all White Papers must include a section containing information on sustainability indicators, in particular with respect to adverse impacts on the climate and other environmental considerations.

IV. Recovery and Redemption Plan

15. Both ART and EMT issuers are subject to the obligation to establish recovery and redemption plans. The content and requirements applicable to such plans are defined by the European Banking Authority (EBA) guidelines,[8] which provide, inter alia, that these plans must be developed with due regard to the equitable treatment of token holders, must not cause undue economic harm, and must ensure the adequate allocation of the reserve of assets to satisfy the token holders' redemption claims. These plans must be implemented in a timely manner and must include clear governance principles governing their preparation, review, update, and execution.

16. The redemption plan must set out a mapping of the critical activities necessary for the orderly implementation of the plan, together with a structured process for redeeming token holders' claims. As for the recovery plan, it must contain predetermined indicators that may trigger the activation of the recovery plan, provide for multiple recovery options and scenarios, specify how the issuer intends to ensure the continuity of its services, and include a communication and disclosure plan directed at token holders.

---

[8] EBA, 'Final Report – Guidelines on Recovery Plans under Articles 46 and 55 of Regulation (EU) 2023/1114', EBA/GL/2024/07, 13 June 2024, [link]; and EBA, 'Final Report – Guidelines on Redemption Plans under Articles 47 and 55 of Regulation (EU) 2023/1114', EBA/GL/2024/13, 9 October 2024, [link].

V. AML/CFT Requirements

17. With regard to anti-money laundering and counter-terrorism financing (AML/CFT) obligations, issuers of EMTs are subject to the relevant AML/CFT framework by virtue of their status as credit or electronic money institutions. Issuers of ARTs are not, however, subject to AML/CFT obligations solely on the basis of issuing ARTs. Nevertheless, they may fall within the scope of AML/CFT rules where they also operate as crypto-asset service providers, in accordance with applicable legislation.

§ 4. ENHANCED SUPERVISION OF SIGNIFICANT STABLECOINS

18. The EBA may classify ARTs and EMTs as significant where certain quantitative or qualitative thresholds are met, including the number of holders, the value in circulation, or the volume of transactions. These thresholds are set out under Article 43, for ARTs, and Article 56, for EMTs, of the MiCA Regulation.

19. Furthermore, the Regulation provides that any issuer of an e-money token authorised as a credit institution or as an electronic money institution may, under certain conditions, voluntarily opt into the regime applicable to issuers of significant e-money tokens. Issuers of significant tokens are subject to enhanced requirements concerning own funds and the reserve of assets, designed to mitigate the systemic risks such tokens may pose to the financial system. These issuers also fall under the supervisory remit of the EBA, which is empowered to impose additional obligations, such as requiring the maintenance of higher own funds or mandating updates to the issuer's recovery and redemption plans.

§ 5. THE COMPLEX OVERLAP OF REGULATORY REGIMES APPLICABLE TO E-MONEY TOKENS

20. EMT issuers currently face legal uncertainty due to the dual nature of e-money tokens. Under the MiCA Regulation, EMTs shall be deemed to be electronic money[9] within the meaning of the Payment Services Directive 2 (PSD2),[10] and are, therefore, subject to the provisions of the PSD2. In this context, certain crypto-asset services as defined under MiCA Regulation – in particular, providing custody and administration of crypto-assets on behalf of

---

9 Art. 48(2), MiCA Regulation states that 'e-money tokens shall be deemed to be electronic money'.

10 Directive (EU) 2015/2366 of the European Parliament and of the Council of 25 November 2015 on payment services in the internal market.

clients, the placing of crypto-assets, and transfer services for crypto-assets on behalf of clients – may overlap with payment services as defined under PSD2. As a result, CASPs offering such services involving EMTs may be required to obtain dual authorisation both as CASPs under the MiCA Regulation and as payment institutions under PSD2. The forthcoming PSD3/R package is expected to address this overlap and prevent unnecessary dual authorisation. Meanwhile, divergent interpretations persist among Member States. In December 2024, the European Commission, together with ESMA, requested that the EBA issue a no-action letter to suspend, on a temporary basis, the obligation for CASPs to obtain Payment Services Providers (PSP) authorisation when EMTs are used solely for investment or trading. Although the EBA committed to publishing this letter by April 2025, it has not yet been released.

SECTION II. THE CHALLENGES ASSOCIATED WITH STABLECOINS

§ 1. CHALLENGES ASSOCIATED WITH GLOBAL STABLECOINS

21. As noted in an October 2020 report by the Financial Stability Board,[11] while stablecoins represent a distinct category of crypto-assets with the potential to enhance the efficiency of financial services provision, they also pose risks to financial stability, particularly if adopted on a large scale. It is important to clarify that no individual stablecoin, nor their collective totality, currently constitutes a systemic risk, especially regarding stablecoins that, by virtue of their features or widespread use, become global in nature rather than confined to a single jurisdiction. This initial challenge has been substantially mitigated within the EU by the implementation of the MiCA Regulation, which prohibits the issuance of stablecoins that fail to comply with its stringent standards.

§ 2. CHALLENGES ASSOCIATED WITH THE MICA REGULATION REQUIREMENTS FOR EUROPEAN CASPS AND ISSUERS

22. Although the MiCA Regulation represents a pioneering regulatory framework, its rigorous implementation imposes strict requirements concerning reserve composition, asset quality, and transparency, including the mandatory submission of detailed White Papers to competent authorities. While these

[11] Financial Stability Board, 'Regulatory, supervisory and oversight challenges raised by global stablecoin arrangements' (2020).

measures aim to protect token holders and reduce systemic risk, they may inadvertently hamper the emergence of competitive euro-denominated stablecoins, potentially disadvantaging European issuers in favour of non-EU counterparts.

§ 3. IMPLICATIONS OF STABLECOINS FOR EUROPEAN MONETARY POLICY

23. The issuance of stablecoins poses profound strategic challenges for the European banking and payments sectors, both economically and legally. As digital instruments backed by fiduciary assets, stablecoins call into question the traditional European monetary architecture, which is built on a two-tier issuance model involving central banks and commercial banks.

24. In September 2020, the ECB Crypto-Asset Task Force highlighted these concerns in its occasional paper series,[12] noting that widespread adoption of stablecoins as a store of value could weaken the central banks' influence over interest rates, reduce banks' deposit bases, increase their funding costs, and impair their lending capacity. Stablecoins backed by high-quality liquid assets may also increase demand for safe assets, potentially restricting their availability for monetary policy operations and complicating liquidity management. The risk of sudden large-scale stablecoin redemptions could exacerbate funding pressures not only for issuers but also for banks and investment funds holding the collateral. Furthermore, multi-currency stablecoins could impact the exchange rate channel of monetary policy, as prices and purchasing power might be influenced by foreign policies and currency fluctuations, complicating domestic monetary objectives and making domestic policy objectives harder to achieve.

§ 4. IMPLICATIONS OF STABLECOINS FOR FINANCIAL STABILITY

25. Stablecoins pose distinct risks to EU financial stability, primarily through liquidity pressures and contagion effects. A sudden loss of confidence could trigger massive redemptions, causing liquidity strains both for stablecoin issuers and the banks holding their collateral. This 'run' risk is heightened if stablecoins are perceived as bank deposit substitutes, potentially destabilising traditional banking liquidity and credit provision.

12 European Central Bank Crypto-Assets Task Force, 'Occasional Paper Series. Stablecoins: Implications for monetary policy, financial stability, market infrastructure and payments, and banking supervision in the euro area', No. 247, September 2020.

26. Moreover, forced asset liquidations to meet redemptions may disrupt short-term government debt markets, increasing volatility and reducing market liquidity. The involvement of banks and financial intermediaries in stablecoin ecosystems further amplifies systemic vulnerabilities, with reputational and operational risks arising alongside financial exposures.

27. The European Systemic Risk Board (ESRB) released on October 2025 a major report highlighting the growing macroprudential implications of crypto-asset markets within the EU. The report identifies three interconnected sources of systemic vulnerability: stablecoins, crypto-investment products, and 'multi-function groups'; and calls for enhanced prudential coordination, stronger enforcement under MiCA, and closer supervisory cooperation across the EU.

28. In sum, the interconnectedness between stablecoins and the traditional financial system creates channels through which shocks could propagate, necessitating robust regulatory oversight to safeguard stability.

§ 5. RISKS POSED BY THE DOMINANCE OF USD-BACKED STABLECOINS

29. From a monetary standpoint, the expansion of stablecoins deepens Europe's reliance on the US dollar. While the euro faces challenges in establishing itself as a key currency within emerging digital payment ecosystems based on distributed ledger technologies, USD-denominated stablecoins have already secured dominance in international trade, currency exchange, and trade finance. Moreover, the growing role of US stablecoins in payment systems threatens the competitiveness of the European payments industry. US payment giants have aggressively acquired fintech firms and formed partnerships with crypto-native companies to embed stablecoins into global payment networks, providing low-cost cross-border transactions alongside innovative consumer and merchant tools.

30. Furthermore, the increasing role of US stablecoins in payment ecosystems risks undermining the competitiveness of the European payments sector. In contrast, Europe remains fragmented, struggling to construct a unified, instant payment solution capable of rivalling dollar-based instruments. Without a coordinated political and industrial response, there is a real danger that both retail users and major corporates will default to using USD-based platforms, marginalising European initiatives. This imbalance poses a threat to European monetary sovereignty by weakening the international role of the euro and undermining its share in global foreign exchange reserves.

31. Ultimately, the controlled development of euro-denominated stablecoins appears not only as a lever for innovation, but as a strategic necessity. It would contribute to financial stability, support the digital transition of the economy, reinforce the euro's international standing, and uphold Europe's sovereignty in the field of digital payments. The current regulatory framework, though ambitious, must evolve in a targeted manner to allow these instruments to emerge without compromising market integrity or the resilience of the banking system. If it does not, Europe risks undergoing, rather than shaping, the ongoing transformation of the global monetary landscape.

CHAPTER 2
FSRA STABLECOIN REGULATION

By Edmond O'Hanlon[1] on 20 February 2025, Symposium *'Regulation of crypto-assets - Comparative law United Arab Emirates / European Union'* at Sorbonne University Abu Dhabi.

SECTION I. OPENING REMARKS

1. It is my pleasure to walk through the FSRA's approach to stablecoins, which we now call 'Fiat-Referenced Tokens' (FRTs), and which we formerly called 'fiat tokens'.

SECTION II. NOT A VIRTUAL ASSET

2. Until very recently, the FSRA referred to stablecoins as 'fiat tokens'; this concept was introduced in the FSRA's Virtual Asset (VA) framework in 2020 for fully fiat-backed single currency stablecoins and clarified that stablecoins were not VAs but instead are a form of 'digital asset'.

3. The FSRA is clear that a fiat token or FRT may be distinguished from a VA by its associated redemption right, whereby a holder may demand a specified amount of fiat currency from the issuer upon the surrender of the token. In contrast, VAs are not backed by any redemption right that obligates the issuer to deliver an agreed amount of fiat currency to a holder upon demand. Instead, the value of VAs fluctuates with their perceived value in the marketplace.

SECTION III. 'FIAT TOKENS' – STORED VALUE

4. Where a fiat token was used as a payment instrument for the purposes of Money Transmission (per the Financial Services and Markets Regulations 2015

---

1 Legal Counsel, Financial Services Regulatory Authority, Abu Dhabi Global Market. All views expressed are the author's views only and do not reflect those of the FSRA, ADGM, or its staff. The FSRA's framework was amended in June and October 2025.

(FSMR))[2], the activity required a licence from the FSRA for Providing Money Services (per FSMR) to use this form of 'Stored Value'; a concept like e-money, in EU parlance.

5. The fiat token issuer was required to *'hold fiat currency'* equal to a portion of the total sum of tokens in issuance. This, however, did not reflect the commercial reality of how stablecoins are actually supported by fiat currency, which is, in fact, with high-quality liquid assets as reserves rather than 100% as funds in a bank account. Rather, the High-quality Liquid Assets (HQLA) which a stablecoin is required to hold to maintain a stable value, can earn some level of return.

6. To date the FSRA has approved 4 stablecoins (or 'fiat tokens') for use in the ADGM on 12 specific blockchain networks. However, to date, none of our firms has needed the Regulated Activity of Providing Money Services for fiat tokens because they were not issuing the stablecoin in the ADGM and they were not themselves using the stablecoin as a 'Payment Instrument' (per FSMR). Instead, the fiat leg of a payment transaction involving fiat tokens would have been handled by an onshore sister company that is a licensed bank.

SECTION IV. 'FIAT-REFERENCED TOKEN' REPLACES 'FIAT TOKEN'

7. Following our Consultation Paper of August 2024,[3] we have a new definition for stablecoins: the 'Fiat-Referenced Token' (FRT). We implemented the necessary changes on 5 December 2024. Now, the issuing or selling of FRTs is no longer considered the issuing or selling of Stored Value, or a form of Providing Money Services. In fact, the issuance of an FRT is now a stand-alone FSRA-regulated activity, separate from Providing Money Services.[4]

8. The FSRA's capital requirements for Stored Value providers (i.e. a variable Capital Requirement of 2.5% of the average daily outstanding stored value over the preceding six months)[5] were considered too restrictive for stablecoin issuers

---

2 See the Financial Services and Markets Regulations 2015 (FSMR): https://en.adgm.thomsonreuters.com/sites/default/files/net_file_store/ADGM1547_12483_VER26020125.pdf.

3 See https://en.adgm.thomsonreuters.com/sites/default/files/net_file_store/Consultation_Paper_No._7_of_2024_FRTs.pdf.

4 However, this is not to say that FRTs are not connected to Payment Services at all. Rather, the following are included amongst the amended Payment Services in FSMR: '(f) the transferring of a Fiat-Referenced Token for the purpose of effecting a Payment Transaction; (g) enabling the settlement of a Payment Transaction effected through the transfer of a Fiat-Referenced Token; (h) the operation of a Payment Account to hold and safeguard Fiat-Referenced Tokens held for the purpose of effecting a Payment Transaction'.

5 See s. 258 of FSMR, and 3.6A.6 of the Prudential – Investment, Insurance Intermediation and Banking Rulebook (PRU): https://en.adgm.thomsonreuters.com/sites/default/files/net_file_store/ADGM1547_11092_VER15020125.pdf.

to be viable or in line with other benchmarked jurisdictions, including the UK, EU, and New York Department of Finance. So, in order to align with the commercial and regulatory realities of how stablecoins are provided elsewhere, and in order to encourage the development of the stablecoin industry within the ADGM, the FSRA introduced the concept of an FRT with prescriptive reserve asset requirements.

9. FSMR has been amended, and a new chapter (Chapter 19A) has been added to the FSRA's 'Conduct of Business Rulebook' (COBS). The definition of an FRT is as follows:

> means a digital asset, the transfer and storage of which is achieved through the use of distributed ledger or similar technology, the purpose of which is to be used as a medium of exchange with a stable store of value, by–
>
> (a) referencing a fixed amount of a single fiat currency; and
>
> (b) enabling the holder to redeem the token in exchange for the amount of the fiat currency referred to in (a) from its issuer upon demand.

10. From this definition it can be derived that algorithmic stablecoins will not be permissible, nor will multi-currency stablecoins or partially backed stablecoins.

11. Algorithmic stablecoins are not permitted by the FSRA. You might recall the implosion of the Terra Luna Stablecoin, which was an algorithmic stablecoin that did not have any collateral to meet redemption requests. Basically, an algorithmic stablecoin is one that does not have sufficient reserves to cover the number of issued tokens. Algorithmic stablecoin issuers use an algorithm to increase or decrease the supply of tokens in order to stabilise its price or reduce volatility in its price and thus attempt to mimic a central bank's monetary policy, but without the means or the legal authority to do so. Given the difficulty of maintaining a robust stabilisation mechanism in the absence of any backing assets with inherent value, issuers of FRTs that derive their value from arbitrage or algorithm will not be granted a licence.

12. Multi-currency stablecoins are not permitted by the FSRA either: an FRT must be a single-currency stablecoin. An FSRA FRT can be used within the ADGM and internationally, subject to local requirements. For example, if an FSRA FRT issuer wanted to have its FRT used in the UAE onshore (i.e. outside the ADGM), it would have to comply with the UAE onshore requirements, which are set out in the CBUAE Payment Token Regulations,[6] and to seek licensing from the Central Bank of the UAE as a 'Foreign Payment Token'.

---

6 See https://rulebook.centralbank.ae/en/rulebook/payment-token-services-regulation.

13. Regarding partially backed stablecoins, unlike the EU's MiCAR,[7] which has the concept of an 'Asset-Referenced Token' (i.e. which could comprise a mixture of fiat, crypto, commodities, etc.), the FSRA does not have a specific definition or class of asset-referenced or commodity-backed stablecoins. For FSRA purposes, commodity-backed stablecoins are not currently recognised. Depending on the mechanics of how the stablecoin was backed, such stablecoins could potentially be recognised under FSMR as either a Spot Commodity or a Commodity Derivative, without requiring an amendment to FSMR to introduce a new category of instrument.[8]

SECTION V. FRTS

14. FRTs are a form of stablecoin backed by HQLA denominated in the same currency as the FRT, that can be liquidated rapidly with minimal adverse price effect.

15. The table below shows that an FRT is a digitally based asset whose purpose is to act as a medium of exchange, and which achieves a stable store of value by referencing a fixed amount of a single fiat currency.

16. It is because each of the boxes can be checked 'yes' that a stablecoin can be recognised by the FSRA as an FRT; all the other items in the table have something missing.

Fiat-Referenced Tokens Compared

			Stablecoins		
	Virtual Asset	**Stored Value**	**FRT**	**Asset-Backed Token**	**Commodity-Backed Token**
Digital Asset	Yes	No	Yes	Yes	Yes
Medium of Exchange	Yes	Yes	Yes	Yes	Yes
Value Set at fixed amount of single fiat currency	No (*Commodity*)	Yes	Yes	No	No (*Digital representation of a commodity*)
Holder can redeem from issuer for fixed amount of fiat currency on demand	No	Yes	Yes	No	No

7 Regulation (EU) 2023/1114 of the European Parliament and of the Council of 31 May 2023 on markets in crypto-assets, and amending Regulations (EU) No. 1093/2010 and (EU) No. 1095/2010 and Directives 2013/36/EU and (EU) 2019/1937: see https://eur-lex.europa.eu/legal-content/EN/TXT/?uri=CELEX%3A02023R1114-20240109.

8 See these definitions in s. 258 of FSMR.

17. Crucially, an FRT gives its holder the right to redeem the FRT from its issuer upon demand in exchange for a specified amount of the fiat currency. You may recall from my previous presentation that the definition of VA that we looked at, amongst other things, includes that it is a digital representation of value that can function as:

(1) a medium of exchange;
(2) and/or a unit of account; or
(3) and/or a store of value.

18. That being the case, what then is the difference between a VA and an FRT? Or, put another way, could an FRT ultimately fit within the definition of a VA? The FSRA's answer to that question is distinctly 'no'; a VA and an FRT are different things entirely from a legal and regulatory perspective. FRTs are intended to be used as a means of payment. An FRT may be distinguished from a VA by its associated redemption right, whereby a holder may demand a specified amount of fiat currency from the issuer upon the surrender of the token. VAs also have investment and speculative purposes, while FRTs do not.

19. While both FRTs and some VAs are used as a medium of exchange, VAs are not backed by any redemption right that obligates the issuer to deliver an agreed amount of fiat currency or other thing of value to a holder upon demand. Without such a redemption right, the market value of a VA fluctuates with the perceived value of the VA in the market. The FSRA regulates VAs as tradeable commodities rather than a security or medium of exchange.

20. Therefore, it is the continuing ability of the issuer to fund a redemption request that establishes a stable value for the token, which in turn facilitates its use as a means of payment. To the extent that a VA is accepted as a medium of exchange, etc., it nonetheless remains a commodity-like instrument that is intermediated and has a privately agreed fluctuating value, and is not a proxy for fiat currency. An FRT can be thought of as either a form of 'money' or having 'monetary value', as it is sufficiently 'money-like'.

SECTION VI. PROHIBITION ON NON-ACCEPTED FRTS

21. The FSRA has prohibited Authorised Persons from issuing, distributing, marketing, making, or accepting as payment any FRT or stablecoin, however described in the ADGM, other than an Accepted Fiat-Referenced Token. You can see that this applies to Authorised Persons, i.e. those licensed by the FSRA. An 'Accepted Fiat-Referenced Token':

> means a Fiat-Referenced Token that, in the opinion of the Regulator, meets the requirements that permit a Regulated Activity to be carried on in relation to it.

22. The FSRA's 'Accepted Fiat-Referenced Token' (AFRT) framework is still to be developed and a list of AFRTs has not yet been published. It remains to be seen whether we should, or could, extend the prohibition against using stablecoins other than an AFRT to all persons in the ADGM, or at least to all persons that are subject to our AML rules, which, as you may have guessed, is wider than just Authorised Persons with an FSRA licence.

23. While we are still working on our AFRT framework, the current guidance in COBS states that the FSRA will recognise AFRTs with reference to the criteria it applies to the recognition of AVAs, the foremost of which is that transactions can be monitored and traced.

24. You can expect that the 4 fiat tokens (on 12 networks) that were not issued in the ADGM, but which have already been approved for use in the ADGM, will be grandfathered over to the new digital assets regime without having to apply for authorisation, so there will not be a cliff-edge effect, but only in respect of the specific blockchain networks for which they have already been assessed.

25. Therefore, the new FRT regime will cover stablecoins issued outside the ADGM and used in the ADGM, and any FRTs that may be issued within the ADGM.

SECTION VII. FRT ISSUANCE AS A REGULATED ACTIVITY

§ 1. APPLICATION AND ONGOING FEES

26. FRT issuers need to be authorised by the FSRA. A USD 70,000 one-off authorisation fee and a further USD 70,000 recurring annual supervision fee apply.

§ 2. YIELD PAYMENTS ON FRT

27. As mentioned, the FSRA's previous concept of a stablecoin (the 'fiat token') came under the rubric of Stored Value which was not permitted to grant interest. Famously, the EU's MiCAR bans interest and benefits on stablecoins, or 'Electronic Money Tokens', as it calls them. In contrast, the FSRA does not prohibit an FRT issuer from accruing and distributing income earned from Reserve Assets to the FRT holder, but the FRT must not be promoted as, nor considered to be, an investment or a savings product. Therefore, yield or interest will be permissible for FSRA FRTs, but it will not be mandatory.

28. The FSRA took the view that the utility of an FRT as an effective medium of exchange is strongly correlated to allowing interest to be paid on it. In order to maintain a stable par value, the interest earned from reserve assets must be accounted for, similar to a money market fund. The issuer must clearly disclose in its White Paper and marketing materials that the payment of any interest or yield from the reserve assets is not as of right. Instead, the payment of interest on an FRT is conditional upon the issuer ensuring that the value of the reserve assets exceeds the par value of the FRT in circulation, and compliance with applicable regulatory requirements at all times.

§ 3. FRT PRUDENTIAL RULES

29. The proposed capital requirement for an FRT issuer will be the higher of either:

- USD 2 million; or
- 12 months of audited expenditure in the form of Tier 1 Capital.[9]

30. However, the main thing is to ensure full backing of all issued tokens, as the primary regulatory concern in relation to FRTs is the ability of the issuer to fund redemption requests in a timely and efficient manner.

31. FRT issuers are required to maintain all proceeds from the issuance of FRTs in:

(a) cash held as 'Relevant Money' in accordance with COBS; and

(b) 'Reserve Investments' comprising admissible high-quality liquid assets denominated in the same currency as the FRT, which can be liquidated rapidly with minimal adverse price effect;

collectively termed 'Reserve Assets'.

§ 4. CASH

32. In contrast to the EU's MiCAR minimum 30% cash deposit requirement for 'stablecoins' (i.e. a bank deposit), the FSRA is of the view that the minimum percentage of cash against the total value of the relevant FRT outstanding should take into account the level of recent and anticipated redemption requests.

33. Instead of prescribing express limits in rules, the FSRA will require applicants to submit their allocation limits in relation to the categories above of eligible Reserve Assets to the FSRA for approval.

---

[9] See the FSRA's PRU Rules 3.3. & 3.7: https://en.adgm.thomsonreuters.com/sites/default/files/net_file_store/ADGM1547_11092_VER15020125.pdf.

§ 5. HIGH-QUALITY LIQUID ASSETS

34. Proceeds from the sale of FRTs can only be invested in HQLA with minimal market, credit, and concentration risk. Reserve Investments[10] means:

(a) cash equivalents and debt securities with up to three-month residual maturity issued by:
   (i) the government or central bank of the jurisdiction of the fiat currency to which the Fiat-Referenced Token is referenced; or
   (ii) organisations that are of both a governmental and an international nature of Credit Quality Grade 1 for CR Exposures;

(b) money-market funds which invest in government debt, subject to Regulator-approved:
   (i) limits on the value of Reserve Investments to be held in such funds; and
   (ii) credit ratings of such funds; and

(c) overnight reverse repurchase agreements over collateralised by debt securities issued by a government or central bank of pegged currency, with a counterparty that is not affiliated with the issuer and is of strong financial standing.

§ 6. VALUED AT MARK-TO-MARKET BASIS DAILY

35. The market value of reserves is to be at least equal to par value of all outstanding FRTs in circulation as of the end of each business day. These are to be valued at mark-to-market (i.e. their current market value) on a daily basis. However, there is also a monthly written attestation requirement to be provided by an independent third party approved by the FSRA.

§ 7. SEGREGATION AND CUSTODY OF RESERVE ASSETS

36. The Reserve Assets must be segregated at all times and held in permitted custodians in the name of clients, as per COBS, to ensure holders' legal right and priority claim of the Reserve Assets in the event of an insolvency of the issuer. Issuers that offer two or more FRTs must operate and maintain segregated pools of Reserve Assets for each FRT. Each of those pools of Reserve Assets must be managed separately.

---

[10] Per the FSRA's Glossary Rulebook (**GLO**). See https://en.adgm.thomsonreuters.com/sites/default/files/net_file_store/ADGM1547_7580_VER21051224.pdf.

§ 8. REPLICATION OF CHAPTER 17 OF COBS

37. An FRT issuer must comply with all applicable regulations and rules for licensed VA firms, including COBS Chapter 17, anti-money laundering and transaction-monitoring requirements (including Travel Rule requirements, where applicable).

§ 9. WHITE PAPER

38. The FSRA's White Paper requirements are not as prescriptive as those of the EU's MiCAR, but cover the essential points of the identity of the issuer, the rights of the token holder, the reserve asset composition and management arrangements, any conditions applicable to redemption 'T+2', and whether or not the FRT will pay interest.

39. As mentioned, an FRT must not be promoted as an investment product or as an interest-bearing savings product. The White Paper must be clear, fair, and not misleading, and presented in a concise and comprehensible form. FRT White Papers must contain a prominent statement that they are not approved by the FSRA, and that the issuer is solely responsible for the White Paper. The FRT issuer must notify the FSRA at least 20 business days before publication of the White Paper.

§ 10. NO OTHER REGULATED ACTIVITIES PERMISSIBLE

40. The FSRA is of the view that the conduct of additional Regulated Activities by an FRT issuer may introduce additional sources of risk which may impair the ability to meet redemption requirements in certain circumstances. Consequently, the FSRA is of the view that an FRT issuer should not be permitted to undertake other Regulated Activities, nor possess an ownership stake in any other entity, to ring-fence and mitigate risks to the FRT issuer. The FSRA would, however, permit such other Regulated Activities to be conducted from related entities, such as a sister company which the FRT issuer does not have a stake in.

41. The provision of other non-issuance services (e.g. lending, staking, dealing) is prohibited. Such other activities can still be conducted from related entities, e.g. a sister company which the issuer does not have a stake in. An issuer cannot have an ownership interest in any other entity.

§ 11. REDEMPTION AT PAR

42. FRT holders must have a right to redeem their FRT at par value with the issuer and have a claim on the Reserve Assets when the issuer is not able to meet redemption obligations. Redemption requests can be made at any time.

43. Redemption conditions (if any) must be reasonable and disclosed upfront (e.g. fees for redemption, ability of the stablecoin holder to onboard successfully with the issuer before redeeming).

44. An FRT issuer must return the par value of the FRT to holders within two business days ('T+2') from a redemption request. In exceptional circumstances, e.g. in times of market stress, the FSRA may direct an issuer to carry out liquidation of the Reserve Investments within a specified period to meet redemption needs, or to allow redemption to extend beyond T+2 if timely redemption would likely jeopardise the Reserve Investments' value or the orderly liquidation of assets.

§ 12. SUBMIT ALLOCATION LIMITS TO THE FSRA FOR APPROVAL

45. Considering that FRT issuance from the ADGM will be a new activity, instead of prescribing express limits in rules, the FSRA proposes to require applicants to submit their allocation limits to the FSRA for approval.

§ 13. STRESS-TEST THE RESERVE ASSETS AGAINST POTENTIAL ADVERSE EVENTS AND MARKET CONDITIONS

46. The FSRA will require at least annual stress tests to demonstrate run scenarios.

Post-speech

Following the speech on 20 February 2025, the FSRA's framework for FRTs was amended in June 2025 with certain changes to FSMR as regards the FSRA's product intervention powers, the applicable fees and prudential rules, and clarifications to COBs on transactions involving FRTs. In September 2025 the FSRA issued a Consultation Paper on key amendments to its FRT framework, including on the eligible criteria for acceptance as an Accepted FRT and the introduction of the concept of 'FRT Intermediation'.[11]

---

[11] See https://en.adgm.thomsonreuters.com/sites/default/files/net_file_store/Consultation_Paper_9_of_2025.pdf.

On 31 October 2025 the FSRA finalised amendments to the regulatory framework, governing activities involving FRTs, following industry consultation. These amendments, effective from 1 January 2026, expand the scope of regulated activities related to FRTs, set out requirements for authorised persons handling FRTs, and clarify the FSRA's approach to accepting FRTs for use in ADGM, with further guidance to be issued.[12]

At that time the FSRA also published its consolidated list of accepted Fiat-Referenced Tokens, containing 7 AFRTs on various networks.[13]

12 See https://www.adgm.com/media/announcements/adgm-fsra-finalises-regulatory-framework-for-regulated-activities-involving-fiat-referenced-tokens.

13 See https://assets.adgm.com/download/assets/AFRT+List+November+2025.pdf/c1b34426b88e11f0912ade26907f67ec.

TITLE 3
OBLIGATIONS OF CRYPTO-ASSETS PLATFORMS, SERVICE PROVIDERS AND CUSTODIANS

CHAPTER 1
THE LEGAL FRAMEWORK GOVERNING THE AUTHORISATION OF CRYPTO-ASSET SERVICE PROVIDERS IN FRANCE PURSUANT TO MICAR

Clément Saudo*

1. Crypto-assets were first regulated in the European Union from the perspective of the prevention of the use of the financial system for the purposes of money laundering or terrorist financing. Directive 2018/843 of 30 May 2018 amending Directive (EU) 2015/849 on the prevention of the use of the financial system for the purposes of money laundering or terrorist financing, known as the 5th AML directive (or AMLD 5),[1] included providers engaged in exchange services between virtual currencies and fiat currencies, as well as custodian wallet providers within the scope of the legal framework for the prevention of the use of the Union financial system for the purposes of money laundering and terrorist financing (AML/CFT). The aim of the European legislator was to enable competent authorities, through the crypto-asset service providers, to monitor what were called, at the time, 'virtual currencies'.[2] In France, this implementation of the AMLD 5 was done through the Pacte Law of 22 May 2019.[3] This law went two steps further than an *ad litteram* implementation of AMLD 5. First, it required digital asset service providers (DASPs) willing to provide these services to be registered with the French *Autorité des marchés financiers* (AMF).[4] This

* This chapter reflects the point of view of its author only. In particular, it does not necessarily represent the views of the AMF on the topic in question.

[1] Directive (EU) 2018/843 of the European Parliament and of the Council of 30 May 2018 amending Directive (EU) 2015/849 on the prevention of the use of the financial system for the purposes of money laundering or terrorist financing, and amending Directives 2009/138/EC and 2013/36/EU.

[2] Recital 8 of AMLD 5.

[3] *Loi n° 2019-486 du 22 mai 2019* [Law 2019-486 of 22 May 2019] *relative à la croissance et la transformation des entreprises.*

[4] More than 90 DASPs were registered as of 15 June 2025 (see the list of registered DASPs: https://www.amf-france.org/fr/espace-epargnants/proteger-son-epargne/listes-blanches).

registration was not a mere record of the digital asset provider but entailed *ex ante* verifications by the AMF of compliance with the AML/CFT regulations, and an examination by the AMF of the good repute and competence of the directors and beneficial owners of the organisation, with the assent of the *Autorité de contrôle prudentiel et de resolution* (ACPR), in relation to the AMF/CFT framework in particular. On this last aspect, this French legal framework evolved further with the adoption of Order 2020-1544 of 9 December 2020[5] strengthening the AMF/CFT framework. This order extended the registration obligation to DASPs that provided services consisting in the exchange of digital assets against other digital assets and the operation of a trading platform for digital assets.[6] Moreover, in addition to this mandatory registration, going further than AMLD 5, the Pacte Law introduced optional licensing under French law.[7] This licence was granted by the AMF.[8] An optionally licensed DASP had to comply with certain requirements in terms of organisation, financial resources, and business conduct, offering more protections to the client. Four service providers obtained optional DASP licences.[9]

2. At the European level, the aim of AMLD 5 was not investor protection nor market integrity. Therefore, before MiCA, the absence of such rules left crypto holders exposed to substantial risks linked to market integrity and market abuses in particular.[10] An overall Union framework for markets in crypto-assets was needed to ensure client protection and market integrity while preventing regulatory fragmentation. Regulation EU 2023/1114 of 31 May 2023 on Markets in crypto-assets (MiCA) entered into force in June 2023. This regulation specifically aims at ensuring that Union legislative acts on financial services provide a comprehensive legislative framework that regulates the issuing of crypto-assets, utility tokens, and also stablecoins (defined as either e-money tokens or asset-referenced tokens), as well as the services provided in respect of crypto-assets. It also enables these crypto-asset service providers to deliver their services throughout the Union, either through the right of establishment or through the freedom to provide services. The provisions applicable to crypto-asset

---

5 *Ordonnance n° 2020-1544 du 9 décembre 2020* [Ordinance 2020-1544 of 9 December 2020] *renforçant le cadre de la lutte contre le blanchiment de capitaux et le financement du terrorisme applicable aux actifs numériques.*

6 Art. L.54-10-2, 3 and 4, of the French Monetary and Financial Code.

7 Ibid., Art. L.54-10-5.

8 Four DASPs were optionally licensed (see the list of optionally licensed DASPs: https://www.amf-france.org/fr/espace-epargnants/proteger-son-epargne/listes-blanches).

9 Arts. L.54-10-5 of the French Monetary and Financial Code and 722-1 *et seq.* of the General Regulations of the AMF. Four DASPs were licensed by the AMF. See the list of licensed DASPs on the AMF website (available at https://www.amf-france.org/en/warnings/white-lists).

10 Recital 4 of MiCA.

service providers (CASPs) became applicable on 30 December 2024.[11] This chapter focuses on this new framework governing the authorisation of CASP. As a preliminary point, the approach adopted by MiCA is to regulate crypto-assets as a separate asset class, distinct, in particular, from financial instruments. This basic premise is worth examining, since some countries have chosen to follow a different approach. This chapter, then, focuses on the authorisation of CASPs: the scope and types of authorisations under MiCA, on the one hand, and the implementation of this authorisation procedure in France, on the other.

SECTION I. GENERAL APPROACH: REGULATION OF CRYPTO-ASSETS AS A SPECIFIC ASSET CLASS

3. 'Crypto-assets' are defined by MiCA as a digital representation of a value or of a right that is able to be transferred and stored electronically using distributed ledger technology or similar technology.[12] The premise on which MiCA is built is that crypto-assets are subject to MiCA because they fall outside the scope of Union legislative acts on financial services, other than those rules in respect of anti-money laundering referred to above. As a consequence, when assessing the characterisation of the activities performed by a service provider, the first step will be to characterise the asset. Some assets transferred and stored electronically using distributed ledger technology or similar technology may not be digital representations of values or rights, or may not have 'financial uses'.[13] Some assets registered on a distributed ledger technology (DLT, e.g. blockchain), therefore, remain outside the scope of MiCA. This is the case for digital art and collectibles. The second consequence is the exclusion from the scope of MiCA of crypto-assets falling within the scope of existing banking and financial regulations. This is the case, in particular, for crypto-assets that qualify as financial instruments; deposits, including structured deposits; and funds, except if they qualify as e-money tokens. Drawing the lines between crypto-assets subject to MiCA and those falling outside of its the scope can be a complicated matter. The European Securities and Markets Authority (ESMA) was, therefore, mandated to issue guidelines on the criteria and conditions for the qualification of crypto-assets as financial instruments. The purpose of these guidelines[14] is to specify criteria for determining whether a crypto-asset qualifies as a financial instrument and,

---

11 Provisions relating to e-money tokens and asset-referenced tokens (Title III and Title IV of MiCA) entered into force and applied from 30 June 2024.

12 Art. 3, para. 1(5) of MiCA.

13 Ibid., recital 10.

14 Guidelines on the conditions and criteria for the qualification of crypto-assets as financial instruments published on 19 March 2025.

therefore, ensuring the common, uniform, and consistent application of the provisions in Article 2(4)(a) of MiCA. Furthermore, these guidelines provide clarification on certain features of utility tokens, NFTs, and hybrid tokens.[15]

4. This regulation of crypto-assets as a separate asset class with a specific regime differs from the approach followed in other geographical areas outside the European Union. Historically, before a bill was passed to regulate stablecoins in the United States,[16] crypto-assets were mainly apprehended in the United States through their characterisations as either commodities or securities, not as a specific asset class.[17] This situation is currently evolving with the adoption of the Genius Act which establishes a regulatory framework specific for payment stablecoins. Moreover, the Digital Asset Market Clarity Act, or Clarity Act, aims at establishing a regulatory framework for 'digital commodities', a specific type of commodities. The bill has passed the Congress and could be discussed by the United States Senate later this year.[18] In the same way, in the United Kingdom, following the entry into force of the Financial Services and Markets Act 2000 (Financial Promotion) (Amendment) Order 2023,[19] the promotion of 'qualifying crypto-assets'[20] was brought within scope of an existing regime – that of 'financial promotion'. Since 8 October 2023, qualifying crypto-assets have been controlled investments and, therefore, fall within the scope of the existing financial promotions regime. In these two countries, crypto-assets are perceived through existing legal characterisations. This shapes the legal status of a given crypto-asset and determines its legal framework and the authorisation necessary to perform the related services.

---

15 Ibid., para. 4.

16 The Guiding and Establishing National Innovation for U.S. Stablecoins Act, or 'GENIUS Act', was signed into law on 18 July 2025.

17 On this topic, see in particular the statement from the US Securities and Exchange Commission (SEC) dated 10 April 2025 on Offerings and Registrations of Securities in the Crypto Asset Markets (available here: https://www.sec.gov/newsroom/speeches-statements/cf-crypto-securities-041025) and the explanations of the US Commodity Futures Trading Commission (CFTC) (available here: https://www.cftc.gov/sites/default/files/idc/groups/public/%40customerprotection/documents/file/oceo_aivc0218.pdf). It should be noted that, on the date of this chapter, on this topic, the Digital Asset Market CLARITY Act advanced in US Congress. It aims at providing clarity on the split of competence between SEC and CFTC on digital assets. The Act would define a 'digital commodity' falling within the scope of the CFTC and would exclude all digital commodities from the definition of a security. The SEC jurisdictions would remain on investment contracts involving a digital commodity.

18 H.R.3633 - Digital Asset Market Clarity Act of 2025.

19 The Financial Services and Markets Act 2000 (Financial Promotion) (Amendment) Order 2023, made 7 June 2023, is available at https://www.legislation.gov.uk/uksi/2023/612/contents/made.

20 Art. 88F of the Financial Services and Markets Act 2000 (Financial Promotion) (Amendment) Order 2023 defines a 'qualifying crypto-asset' as a crypto-asset which is: (a) fungible; and (b) transferable. The circumstances in which a crypto-asset is to be treated as 'transferable' include where: (a) it confers transferable rights; or (b) a communication made in relation to the crypto-asset describes it as being transferable or conferring transferable rights.

SECTION II. AUTHORISATION PROCEDURES APPLICABLE TO CASPS UNDER MICA

5. Once the characterisation as a crypto-asset has been confirmed, the second step will be to determine whether the activities performed by an undertaking require an authorisation. First, where crypto-asset services are provided in a fully decentralised manner without any intermediary, they would not fall within the scope of MiCA.[21] Furthermore, the activities performed by the service provider have to be one of the services subject to authorisation,[22] and to be performed within the European Union.[23] Ten crypto-asset services listed in MiCA[24] require prior authorisation when rendered within the European Union. Two types of authorisation exist: an authorisation pursuant to Article 63 of MiCA or a notification pursuant to Article 60 of MiCA.[25]

6. Authorisation is a two-step process. Competent authorities must first check whether the application is complete and may refuse to review applications where such applications remain incomplete after the expiry of the applicable deadline.[26] Then the competent authorities must review the application file and may refuse authorisation as a crypto-asset service provider where there are objective and demonstrable grounds that the management body or shareholders of the applicant CASP pose a threat to its effective, sound, and prudent management and business continuity, or do not meet the criteria of sufficiently good repute set out in MiCA, or if the applicant CASP fails to meet or is likely to fail to meet any of the requirements of MiCA.[27]

7. A simplified notification procedure is available to certain financial entities: credit institutions, central securities depositories, market operators, investment firms, electronic money institutions, and management companies. Since their status already requires them to comply with demanding rules, they may provide crypto-asset services without authorisation as a crypto-asset service provider

---

21 Recital 22 and Art. 140 of MiCA.

22 Art. 2 of MiCA defines the scope of the persons and crypto-activities services subject to MiCA.

23 Art. 61 of MiCA defines the situations where the provision of crypto-asset services is rendered at the exclusive initiative of the client, the crypto-asset service then being deemed to be rendered outside the European Union.

24 The ten crypto-asset services are: providing custody and administration of crypto-assets on behalf of clients (1); operation of a trading platform for crypto-assets (2); exchange of crypto-assets for funds within the meaning of MiCA or for other crypto-assets (3 and 4); execution of orders for crypto-assets on behalf of clients (5); placing of crypto-assets (6); reception and transmission of orders for crypto-assets on behalf of clients (7); providing advice on crypto-assets (8); providing portfolio management on crypto-assets (9); and providing transfer services for crypto-assets on behalf of clients (10).

25 Art. 59 of MiCA.

26 Ibid., Art. 63, para. 3.

27 Ibid., Art. 60, para. 8.

under MiCA, if they provide their competent authorities with certain information before providing those services for the first time. Once this notification procedure is completed, they are subject to all requirements applicable to CASP under MiCA, with the exception of authorisation requirements, own funds requirements, and the approval procedure regarding shareholders and members that have qualifying holdings. Those matters are already covered by the respective legislative acts under which these financial entities are authorised. CASPs benefiting from the notification procedure may render crypto-asset services equivalent to those they are authorised to provide under their original status, with the exception of credit institutions authorised to provide all crypto-asset services. Moreover, financial entities may always request an authorisation for services not covered by the equivalence. Candidates have to provide certain information generally equivalent to that required in the context of the authorisation process. The national competent authority is then in charge of verifying the completeness of the application file.[28] This is not only a quantitative assessment but also a qualitative one. National competent authorities would, therefore, check the quality of the documents, information, and procedures provided. In case of incompleteness, they would inform the applicant of such incompleteness and set a deadline by which that entity is required to provide the missing information.[29]

SECTION III. IMPLEMENTATION OF THE AUTHORISATION PROCEDURES IN FRANCE

8. Pursuant to Article 143 of MiCA, CASPs that provided their services in accordance with applicable law before 30 December 2024 could benefit from a transitional period. This was an option left to Member States. France has implemented a transition period of 18 months.[30] As a consequence, French digital asset service providers who can demonstrate that they provided services in accordance with the applicable national law before that date may continue to do so for a maximum period of 18 months, until 1 July 2026. This provision applies until they are granted or refused authorisation under MiCA. Similar to the registration of DASPs under the Pacte Law, the authorisation process of a CASP involves both the AMF and the ACPR. The authorisation as a CASP in accordance with Article 63 of MiCA in France is granted by the AMF, with the assent of the ACPR in relation to the applicant CASP's internal control mechanisms, policies, and procedures for identifying, assessing, and managing

[28] Ibid., Art. 60, para. 3.

[29] Ibid.

[30] See Art. 8 of Law n°2023-171 of 9 March 2023.

risks, including money laundering and terrorist financing risks.[31] The ACPR also provides an opinion on the compliance with fit and proper requirements applicable to the management body and to the shareholders or members that have qualifying holdings of the applicant CASP.[32] In relation to a notified CASP, the authority responsible for the original status of the financial entity will generally be in charge of the authorisation process. Therefore, a central securities depository, a market operator, or a management company may render crypto-asset services if it notifies the AMF of the information referred to in Article 60(7) of MiCA.[33] A credit institution, an investment firm,[34] or an electronic money institution must notify the ACPR of the same information before starting to provide the crypto-asset services. A crypto-asset service provider that intends to passport its crypto-asset services in other Member States must inform the AMF or the ACPR, as the case may be, of its intent. A list of CASPs authorised in France is published by the AMF. More generally, ESMA will establish a register of crypto-asset service providers.

9. The AMF may withdraw the authorisation of a CASP pursuant to Article 64 of MiCA following a request from the CASP, on its own initiative or on the initiative of the ACPR, based on Article 64(1)(f)(f), or Article 64(2) of the same regulation on the initiative of the ACPR.[35] In relation to notified CASPs, logically, their ability to render crypto-asset services will be dependent on their underlying authorisation as a financial entity. Their rights to provide crypto-asset services will be revoked upon the withdrawal of the relevant authorisation that enabled the relevant entity to provide the crypto-asset services without being required to obtain an authorisation.[36] Once authorised, the supervision of a CASP will then be performed by the ACPR and the AMF. In relation to a CASP authorised in accordance with Article 63 of MiCA, the supervision will be performed by the AMF,[37] except in relation to the AML/CFT requirements, which will be supervised by the ACPR.[38] In relation to CASPs notified in accordance with Article 60 of MiCA, a central securities depository, a market operator, or a management company will be supervised by the AMF. A credit institution, an investment firm, or an electronic money institution will be supervised by the ACPR, except in relation to the conduct rules, which will be the supervised by the AMF.

---

31 Art. L54-10-7 of the French Monetary and Financial Code.

32 These assents and opinions are not rendered by the ACPR when the candidate is a portfolio management company or intends to render only the services of advice on crypto-assets or portfolio management on crypto-assets, or both of these two services.

33 Art. L.54-10-7 III of the French Monetary and Financial Code.

34 Other than a management company.

35 Art. L.54-10-7 IV of the French Monetary and Financial Code.

36 Art. 60(11) of MiCA.

37 Art. L.621-9 of the French Monetary and Financial Code.

38 Ibid., Art. L.612-2.

10. In order to organise the transition to MiCA, in October 2024 French law was modified,[39] not only to define the competent authorities mentioned above, but also to clarify the legal nature and define the proprietary aspects of crypto-assets under French law. Following this, the AMF updated its general regulations to provide clarity on the authorisation process. In particular, further details were given on the benefit of the transitional period and the scope of the activities of eligible market participants and the legal framework applicable during this transitional period. Since 1 July 2024, it has been possible to apply for authorisation to the AMF to become a crypto-asset service provider, with a view to pre-examination by the AMF. The first authorisations have been granted by the AMF during the first semester of 2025.[40] The transitional period in France will end on 1 July 2026. This means that French registered DASPs will have the necessary time to transition to the new CASP regime.

39 Order n°2024-936 dated 15 October 2024 relating to the market in crypto-assets.

40 The list of CASPs authorised to render crypto-asset services in France can be found on the website of the AMF (https://www.amf-france.org/en/warnings/white-lists). The list of CASPs authorised to render crypto-asset services in the European Union can be found on the ESMA website (https://www.esma.europa.eu/esmas-activities/digital-finance-and-innovation/markets-crypto-assets-regulation-mica#InterimMiCARegister).

CHAPTER 2

COMPARATIVE ANALYSIS OF THE EU MICAR AND THE VARA REGULATORY REGIME FOR VIRTUAL ASSETS

Maria Luisa BABO RODRIGUES, Diego MONTES SERRALDE, Nicholas MCNICHOLAS, and Ruben BOMBARDI

SECTION I. EXECUTIVE SUMMARY

1. This chapter offers a comparative overview of two major regulatory frameworks for digital assets: the European Union (EU)'s MiCAR and Dubai's VARA regime. While both frameworks share core principles, such as market integrity, transparency, and proportionality, they diverge in design and regulatory philosophy. MiCAR emphasises consistency and cross-border integration within the EU, whereas VARA prioritises flexibility and innovation through a locally centralised model, offering tailored oversight for emerging technologies like DeFi and tokenised Real World Assets (RWAs). Key points of comparison include:

Category	VARA	MiCAR
Taxonomy and classification	VARA sets out the framework for broader asset categories with unique regulatory implications, including a dedicated regime for tokenised RWAs under the ARVA framework.	MiCAR classifies crypto-assets (CAs) as EMTs, ARTs, and utility tokens.
Prudential requirements	Require capital buffers and asset segregation. VARA focuses on liquidity and accessibility under the custody of financial institutions licensed or authorised to provide services in the UAE.	Require capital buffers and asset segregation. MiCAR prescribes rules for capital composition based on EU banking standards

AML/CFT	VARA's framework is sector-specific but leverages federal AML/CFT legislation and international best standards. Follows FATF Recommendations.	MiCAR leverages the EU's general AML/CFT regime, with variable specificities according to national implementation. Follows FATF Recommendations.
Information technology	VARA imposes tailored cybersecurity, key management, and smart contract audit requirements, recently strengthened through detailed Guidelines issued on 19 June 2025.	MiCAR subjects crypto-asset service providers to the Regulation on Digital Operational Resilience (DORA), mandating ICT risk frameworks, incident reporting, and penetration testing.
Virtual Asset Issuance	VARA requires detailed White Papers, reserve asset disclosures, and licensing for Category 1 issuances (FRVAs/ARVAs), with a licensed-distribution-only regime for Category 2 VAs.	MiCAR mandates authorisation and disclosures for ARTs/EMTs and sets lighter rules for other CAs.
Governance	Both regimes mandate clear governance structures, policies, and fit and proper standards for management and key function holders.	
Market conduct	Both frameworks impose strict rules on market abuse, fair marketing, and investor protection.	
Enforcement and supervision	VARA centralises regulatory control within a single, agile body tailored to Dubai's evolving Virtual Asset (VA) landscape.	MiCAR emphasises harmonisation across the EU and coordination among multiple authorities.

SECTION II. INTRODUCTION

2. This chapter examines key regulatory requirements for crypto-assets and Virtual Asset Service Providers (CASPs or VASPs) based on MiCAR and the regulatory regime from VARA.[1] Pursuant to its regulatory powers, VARA issued a dedicated set of regulations: the Virtual Assets and Related Activities Regulations 2023 (VARA Regulations 2023), the Regulations on the Marketing of Virtual Assets and Related Activities 2024 (Marketing Regulations), and two

[1] The legal framework for virtual assets (VA) services in the United Arab Emirates is laid out in Cabinet Decision No. 111/2022 on the Regulation of Virtual Assets and their service providers ('CD 111') and Cabinet Decision No. 112/2022 on Delegating Certain Competencies related to the Regulation of Virtual Assets ('CD 112'). Law no. (4) of 2022 Regulating Virtual Assets in the Emirate of Dubai ('Law no. 4') lays down the legal framework for the establishment of VARA and sets out its mandate, responsibilities, and powers to pursue them.

sets of rule books: the Compulsory Rulebooks[2] and the VA-Activity and Other Rulebooks.[3]

3. The objective of this analysis is to highlight key similarities and differences in both approaches to regulating VASPs in this rapidly evolving market. The research is based solely on the information contained within the above-mentioned regulatory provisions and does not entail providing any judgement on the content, applicability, or enforceability of such regimes.

SECTION III. COMPARATIVE ANALYSIS

§ 1. OVERVIEW

4. The regulatory approach, objectives, and target audience of the MiCAR and VARA frameworks reflect different policy philosophies shaped by their respective jurisdictions. MiCAR adopts a product-centric and harmonisation-driven approach, aiming to provide legal certainty across the EU by regulating crypto-assets based on their classification (namely asset-referenced tokens, e-money tokens, and other crypto-assets). MiCAR's primary objective is to ensure consumer protection, market integrity, and financial stability, thereby addressing regulatory fragmentation across the EU. MiCAR sets out the high-level framework and minimum mandatory requirements that all CASPs in the EU must adhere to, as well as the minimum faculties that all national competent authorities for licensing and supervising CASPs must be equipped with. EU regulations do not require national transposition and are directly applicable in all EU Member States, and thus must allow for sufficient flexibility for adequate implementation in national markets and regulatory environments that may have significant differences. This high-level framework is developed both through Regulatory and Implementing Technical Standards developed by the European Banking Authority (EBA) and the European Securities and Markets Authority (ESMA), and through national regulations issued by the competent authorities. The competent authorities for licensing and supervising CASPs will be defined at the national level, with the EBA retaining power to approve issuance of certain significant crypto-assets, as outlined in more detail below, due to their greater potential risks to financial stability.

2 Comprising the Company Rulebook, Compliance and Risk Management Rulebook, Technology and Information Rulebook, and Market Conduct Rulebook ('Compulsory Rulebooks').

3 Comprising the Advisory Services Rulebook, Broker-Dealer Services Rulebook, Custody Services Rulebook, Exchange Services Rulebook, Lending and Borrowing Services Rulebook, Management and Investment Services Rulebook, Transfer and Settlement Services Rulebook, and Virtual Asset Issuance Rulebook ('VA-Activity Rulebooks').

5. In contrast, VARA employs an activity-based, innovation-led regulatory model, focusing on the specific VA activities being performed, regardless of the underlying asset classification. VARA's objective is to establish the Emirate of Dubai as a global hub for VAs by promoting responsible innovation, fostering regulatory clarity, and facilitating experimental business models such as DeFi protocols and tokenised real estate. VARA's regulatory framework follows a principle-based approach, opting to set out the regulatory objectives and outcomes that VASPs must achieve rather than how these must be achieved, and ensuring through VARA's supervisory mandate that VASPs implement efficient and adequate systems, controls, policies, and procedures to meet these objectives and outcomes. Finally, VARA is the single regulator in the Emirate of Dubai only, although, once licensed, its VASPs may provide services throughout the UAE,[4] and VARA closely cooperates with other competent authorities both at the domestic and foreign level.

§ 2. TAXONOMY AND CLASSIFICATION OF VAS

6. Pursuant to Law No. 4, VARA introduced the concept of 'Virtual Tokens'[5] as the first concept related to the crypto sector, which includes the definition of a 'Virtual Asset' (VA) as a 'digital representation of value that may be digitally traded, transferred, or used as an exchange or payment tool, or for investment purposes'.

7. From a taxonomy perspective, VARA includes three distinct categories that stem from the main concept of VA: (i) Fiat-referenced Virtual Assets (FRVAs); (ii) Asset-referenced Virtual Assets (ARVAs); and (iii) Exempt Virtual Assets (Exempt VAs):

- An *FRVA* is a VA that purports to maintain a stable value in relation to the value of one or more fiat currencies, or one or more other FRVAs, but does not have legal tender status in the UAE and is not issued for use as a means of payment for goods or services in the UAE.
- An *ARVA* is a VA which: (i) represents, or purports to represent, direct, indirect, current, future or contingent ownership of any Real-World Asset (RWA); (ii) represents, or purports to represent, direct, indirect, current, future or contingent entitlement to receive or share any income; (iii) purports to

[4] The UAE Securities and Commodities Authority (SCA) is the competent authority for approving and licensing VA activities in the UAE at the federal level. These powers may be delegated to Local Licensing Authorities (LLAs), which are vested with the authority to regulate VAs in the emirate concerned. VARA is the LLA for the Emirate of Dubai. There is *automatic* mutual recognition between *licences granted by* SCA and VARA, *upon their registration.*

[5] A Virtual Token is defined as, 'A digital representation of a set of rights that can be digitally offered and traded through a Virtual Asset Platform.'

maintain a stable value or reference to any type or combination of RWA(s) or income; (iv) represents, or purports to represent, an entitlement to receive or share any value that is, or purports to be, or in any manner originates from, is derived from or backed by (including but not limited to under any securitisation, collateralisation, or guarantee arrangement) any type or combination of RWA or income; or (v) is a directly or indirectly wrapped, duplicated, fractionalised, securitised, or derivative version of any other ARVA.

- *Exempt* VA is categorised as any VA which does not constitute an FRVA or an ARVA and is either: (i) a Non-Transferable VA;[6] (ii) a Redeemable Closed-Loop VA;[7] or (iii) any other VA as may be determined by VARA from time to time.

8. Similarly, MiCAR provides a general 'catch-all' definition of Crypto Assets (CAs) as 'a digital representation of a value or of a right that is able to be transferred and stored electronically using distributed ledger technology or similar technology'. From this definition, three main categories are regulated:

- *Electronic Money Tokens (EMTs)*: a type of CA that purports to maintain a stable value by referencing the value of one official currency.
- *Asset-referenced Tokens (ARTs)*: a type of CA that is not an EMT and that purports to maintain a stable value by referencing another value or right or a combination thereof, including one or more official currencies.
- *Utility tokens*: a type of CA that is only intended to provide access to a good or a service supplied by its issuer.[8]

9. From these categories, we can infer two main differences: (i) VARA considers VAs that purport to maintain a stable value in relation to the value

---

6 'means a Virtual Asset that—,
(a) is not sold by the Issuer for, and cannot be converted into, exchanged or redeemed for, fiat currency, Virtual Assets or any value in kind;
(b) is not redeemable or exchangeable for goods, services, discounts, purchases or otherwise has no market, use, or application; and
(c) cannot be transferred between VA Wallets.'

7 'means a Virtual Asset that can be redeemed or exchanged for goods, services, discounts, or purchases with the Issuer and/or other merchants designated by the Issuer, provided that—,
(a) the Issuer is the legal owner and/or has validly enforceable legal right to grant all rights of redemption;
(b) the Virtual Asset is not sold or exchanged for, and cannot be converted into, exchanged or redeemed for, fiat currency or Virtual Assets;
(c) cannot be used or accepted as a means of payment outside of the closed-loop of the Issuer and/or other merchants designated by the Issuer; and
(d) cannot be transferred between VA Wallets other than for the purposes of redemption from the Issuer or designated merchants.'

8 While utility tokens are considered crypto-assets for the purposes of MiCAR, and thus fall under its regulatory scope, MiCAR requirements do not apply to crypto-assets (excluding asset-referenced and e-money tokens) that are offered for free, created as rewards through consensus mechanisms, or are utility tokens used to access existing goods or services, especially within a limited merchant network.

of one or more fiat currencies as FRVAs, while MiCAR differentiates between EMTs and ARTs based on the underlying asset being stable in relation to one (in the case of EMTs) or more (in the case of ARTs) fiat currencies or other assets; (ii) VARA considers a special category for the so-called 'RWA tokens' due to the growing tokenisation industry, while MiCAR does not have a specific category to regulate these types of asset, generating those assets to be treated as general CAs.

§ 3. RESTRICTIONS OR OUT-OF-SCOPE VAS

10. VARA and MiCAR identify specific restrictions and exclusions of VAs/CAs. These restrictions or exclusions apply in two scenarios: (i) the VA/CA itself has characteristics that allow entities to avoid compliance controls and, therefore, should be restricted; or (ii) the VA/CA is regulated in its entirety by another regulatory framework and, therefore, falls outside the regulatory scope of the regulator.

I. Restrictions

11. VARA imposes a blanket restriction on the issuance and trade of Anonymity Enhanced Cryptocurrencies (AEC), which mean any type of VA that prevents the tracing of transactions or record of ownership through distributed public ledgers and for which the VASP has no mitigating technologies or mechanisms to allow traceability or identification of ownership. The same restrictions apply in MiCAR, which states that CASPs shall prevent the admission to trading of CAs that have an inbuilt anonymisation function unless the holders of those crypto-assets and their transaction history can be identified by the CASP operating a trading platform for CAs.

II. Out of Scope

12. MiCAR explicitly excludes from its scope 'crypto-assets that are unique and not fungible with other crypto-assets', known as non-fungible tokens (NFTs), which are not regulated under MiCAR, except in cases where the NFTs function like asset-referenced tokens, e-money tokens, or utility tokens. MiCAR would also not apply to any digital assets issued by central banks acting in their monetary authority capacity, including central bank money in digital form, or crypto-assets issued by other public authorities, including central, regional, and local administrations.

13. In contrast, VARA treats NFTs as VAs under its framework, and similarly excludes from its scope the so-called Central Bank Digital Currencies (CBDCs) and the issuance of UAE dirham-backed FRVAs. Both CDBCs and

UAE dirham-backed FRVAs shall remain under the sole and exclusive regulatory purview of the Central Bank of the United Arab Emirates (CBUAE).

§ 4. REQUIREMENTS FOR CASPS/VASPS

14. VARA regulates Virtual Asset Service Providers (VASPs), which are entities licensed by VARA to conduct, by way of business, any of the following VA activities: advisory, broker-dealer, custody, exchange, lending and borrowing, management and investment, transfer and settlement, and issuance of VAs.

15. In comparison, a Crypto-Asset Service Provider (CASP), under the MiCAR regime, is defined as 'a legal person or other undertaking whose occupation or business is the provision of one or more crypto-asset services to clients on a professional basis'.[9] MiCAR applies uniform requirements to CASPs engaged in the issuance, offer, and admission to trading of CAs, or in providing CA services.

16. In the following sections, we provide a brief explanation and description of the general requirements applicable to VASPs/CASPs under the VARA and MiCAR regimes.

§ 5. PRUDENTIAL REQUIREMENTS

17. VARA and MiCAR both impose a prudential framework that follows internationally accepted standards, requiring VASPs and CASPs to have in place several prudential safeguards to ensure their financial soundness, solvency, and liquidity.

I. Capital Requirements

18. VARA and MiCAR adopt a similar approach to the stipulation of minimum capital requirements for VASPs and CASPs.[10] Both regulatory frameworks determine the minimum capital requirements based on the types

---

9 Art. 3(16) defines 'crypto-asset service' as any of the following services and activities relating to any crypto-asset: '(a) providing custody and administration of crypto-assets on behalf of clients; (b) operation of a trading platform for crypto-assets; (c) exchange of crypto-assets for funds; (d) exchange of crypto-assets for other crypto-assets; (e) execution of orders for crypto-assets on behalf of clients; (f) placing of crypto-assets; (g) reception and transmission of orders for crypto-assets on behalf of clients; (h) providing advice on crypto-assets; (i) providing portfolio management on crypto-assets; (j) providing transfer services for crypto-assets on behalf of clients.'

10 These capital requirements may be found in Annex IV of MiCAR and Part VI.B. of the VARA Company Rulebook, respectively.

of services VASPs/CASPs provide, and both requirements are determined as the higher of a fixed amount or a percentage of fixed annual overheads.[11] A key difference arises in terms of capital composition, as VARA does not specifically prescribe composition requirements for paid-up capital, but rather stipulates that it must always be maintained either in a trust account with a licensed UAE bank or through a perpetual surety bond from an authorised UAE company, in both cases with VARA as beneficiary, or in any other manner specified by VARA upon licensing. In contrast, MiCAR requires that minimum capital requirements be met with Common Equity Tier 1 (CET 1) items.[12]

19. VARA regulations place emphasis on holding paid-up capital in secure, accessible forms, indicating a pragmatic, asset-protection-oriented approach, prioritising liquidity and local oversight, and MiCAR follows a similar approach to that of traditional financial institutions, adopting a prudential, risk-based approach aligned with the EU's banking standards.

II. Safeguarding Requirements and Segregation of Client Assets

20. Safeguarding and asset segregation requirements under MiCAR and VARA reflect differing levels of prescriptiveness and supervisory emphasis but are aligned on the final objective. MiCAR imposes detailed and harmonised obligations on CASPs to safeguard clients' CAs and funds with a qualified custodian (i.e. a bank), mandating strict segregation of client assets from the firm's own assets and requiring robust custody arrangements to prevent commingling and misuse.

21. Similarly, VARA safeguarding requirements impose on VASPs the obligation to maintain client assets with a UAE-based bank and require VASPs to maintain a functional segregation of client assets between each other and with the VASP's proprietary assets. In addition to client money segregation, VASPs providing custody services must segregate the VAs of each client in separate VA wallets containing only that client's assets, in order to avoid commingling and insolvency procedures negatively affecting clients' VAs.

III. Financial Statements

22. VARA requires VASPs to submit detailed monthly financial statements (balance sheet, P&L, income, cash flow, VA Wallet addresses), quarterly

---

[11] Ranging from approximately USD 30,000 to USD 410,000 in the VARA Regulations, and from USD 60,000 and EUR 175,000 in MiCAR, or as 15% or 25% of fixed annual overheads.

[12] Consisting of qualifying capital instruments and related share premiums, as well as retained earnings, accumulated other comprehensive income, other reserves, and general banking risk funds, provided they are fully available to the CASP for immediate and unrestricted use to absorb risks or losses.

reports (capital, reserves, projections, risk report), and annual audited financial statements. In the case of MiCAR, it does not prescribe such detailed reporting requirements, since MiCAR is an EU-wide regulation, thus providing national competent authorities with discretion to establish their own reporting requirements. As an example of a national framework for submission of financial statements following MiCAR's overarching requirements, the Malta Financial Services Authority (MFSA) requires CASPs to provide to the supervisor key financial statements, including an income statement and balance sheet, with a frequency of three, six, and nine months, complemented by an audited annual financial statement confirmed by an external auditor.

§ 6. AML/CFT REQUIREMENTS YIELD-BEARING

23. VARA has a dedicated Compliance and Risk Management Rulebook[13] with a full suite of provisions dedicated to the prevention of money laundering, terrorism financing (AML/CFT), proliferation financing, and sanctions non-compliance. In addition, VARA explicitly requires compliance with other relevant federal legislation and international guidelines for AML/CFT, explicitly including FATF Standards on Virtual Assets and VASPs.[14] On the other hand, MiCAR mandates that CASPs comply with the applicable EU AML-CFT framework, which is a broad framework that comprises an AML/CFT Regulation[15] and Directive,[16] as well as a Transfer of Funds Regulation[17] dedicated to setting the rules for compliance with the travel rule.

24. VARA regulation and the EU AML framework impose similar obligations to VASPs/CASPs in the remit of AML/CFT and are aligned with internationally recognised standards in the obligations they impose on their supervised entities. These include obligations for VASPs and CASPs to: (i) have in place AML/CFT policies, procedures, systems, and controls; (ii) employ customer due diligence (CDD) measures before and during the establishment of a business relationship or before conducting a transaction for a non-client, as well as to use enhanced

13 https://rulebooks.vara.ae/rulebook/compliance-and-risk-management-rulebook.

14 https://www.fatf-gafi.org/en/topics/virtual-assets.html.

15 Regulation (EU) 2024/1624 of the European Parliament and of the Council of 31 May 2024 on the prevention of the use of the financial system for the purposes of money laundering or terrorist financing.

16 Directive (EU) 2015/849 of the European Parliament and of the Council of 20 May 2015 on the prevention of the use of the financial system for the purposes of money laundering or terrorist financing, amending Regulation (EU) No. 648/2012 of the European Parliament and of the Council, and repealing Directive 2005/60/EC of the European Parliament and of the Council and Commission Directive 2006/70/EC.

17 Regulation (EU) 2023/1113 of the European Parliament and of the Council of 31 May 2023 on information accompanying transfers of funds and certain crypto-assets and amending Directive (EU) 2015/849.

CDD for high-risk clients or politically exposed persons (PEPs); (iii) continuously monitor VA transactions and VA wallet addresses, and specifically to screen for and report suspicious transactions; (iv) conduct AML/CFT business risk assessments and client risk assessments with periodic updating frequency; and (v) comply with the travel rule for VA and CA transfers with a value exceeding the equivalent to approximately USD 1,000, for which VASPs/CASPs must obtain or send a minimum set of information about the sender and recipient of the transfer of VAs.

25. The approach to the 'sunrise issue' (i.e. how to supervise transfers originating from VASPs/CASPs or non-supervised entities that do not comply with the travel rule) differs, with VARA following a principle-based approach and the EU framework following a more prescriptive approach. Due diligence on counterparty VASPs is required under the VARA regulation, as well as a plan to ensure compliance with the travel rule when dealing with VASPs in jurisdictions where the travel rule is not a legislative requirement. The EU framework also requires CASPs to conduct due diligence on cross-border correspondent relationships with CASPs not established in the EU and specifically foresees an obligation for CASPs to either reject or suspend a transaction which does not comply with the travel rule requirements, and to consider restricting or terminating a business relationship in the case of repeated failures to provide the information required under the travel rule.

26. A significant difference emerges between these regulatory frameworks, as the VARA AML/CFT framework is designed specifically for VAs. For instance, VARA specifically anticipates the obligation for VASPs to use distributed ledger analytics tools to manage AML/CFT risks in the context of transaction monitoring. In the case of MiCAR, the EU AML/CFT framework is applicable and specifies that different national competent authorities will have the responsibility to supervise VASPs' compliance with AML/CFT requirements, and specific obligations tailored to the VA operational reality may be contemplated at the national level only. For instance, the Portuguese dedicated AML-CFT national regulation[18] for CASPs mandates supervised entities to specifically employ decentralised ledger analytics tools for CDD.

[18] Aviso do Banco de Portugal No. 1/2023.

§ 7. TECHNOLOGY AND INFORMATION REQUIREMENTS

27. All CASPs as defined under MiCAR are subject to DORA,[19] which imposes EU-wide standards for digital operational resilience. This includes requirements for ICT risk management frameworks, policies and procedures, including mandatory incident reporting, information sharing on cyber threats, resilience testing, and oversight of third-party providers. VARA, by contrast, has issued a dedicated Technology and Information Rulebook[20] tailored to VASPs' operational reality, covering similar areas but with sector-specific detail. It requires VASPs to implement a technology governance and risk assessment framework, address cybersecurity objectives and controls, and have a dedicated incident management framework. Some requirements tailored to the VA sector relate to the generation, signing, storage, and access of cryptographic keys and VA wallets, requiring industry best practices like preventing single points of failure and using multi-signature approaches. VASPs must also adopt procedures to prevent automated system manipulation. In June 2025, VARA further clarified these expectations through a detailed guideline, strengthening the foundational framework of VARA's regulatory regime by detailing the minimum requirements for IT infrastructure resilience, incident response protocols, encryption standards, and third-party service oversight, including cloud and wallet providers.

I. Stress-testing

28. Entities subject to DORA, including CASPs, should regularly test their ICT systems, and staff with ICT-related responsibilities, to uncover and address potential ICT vulnerabilities. DORA prescribes a minimum frequency of three years for entities to conduct advanced testing of their operational resilience by means of test-led penetration testing (TLPT). The VARA Technology and Information Rulebook requires all VASPs to engage qualified, independent third-party auditors to perform vulnerability assessments annually and before introducing new systems, applications, or products. VASPs must also maintain effective internal monitoring and regularly conduct security and vulnerability audits on both internal and external systems. Finally, VARA may also require VASPs to conduct TLPT using external testers where it considers it necessary and proportionate to do so.

---

19 Regulation (EU) 2022/2554 of the European Parliament and of the Council of 14 December 2022 on digital operational resilience for the financial sector and amending Regulations (EC) No. 1060/2009, (EU) No. 648/2012, (EU) No. 600/2014, (EU) No. 909/2014 and (EU) 2016/1011.

20 https://rulebooks.vara.ae/rulebook/technology-and-information-rulebook.

II. Disaster Recovery Planning / Business Continuity Planning (BCDR)

29. Both MiCAR and VARA Regulations contemplate the need for CASPs and VASPs to have in place procedures designed to ensure the continued availability and prompt restoration of essential operations and IT systems following disruption. VARA requires all VASPs to implement, maintain, test, and annually update an adequate BCDR plan to minimise operational disruption in the case of trigger events, such as cybersecurity events and technical failures. In the EU, however, all CASPs are subject to the provisions of DORA, and MiCAR specifically requires as an authorisation requirement that ART issuers establish BCDR policies to preserve or promptly restore essential data and functions in case of ICT disruptions, while also implementing and regularly reviewing robust internal controls and risk management procedures to ensure the adequacy and effectiveness of their ICT safeguards.

III. Cyber Incidents/Notification Requirements for Systemic Events

30. Under the EU framework,[21] CASPs must submit an initial report as early as possible within four hours from the moment of classification of the incident as major, and no later than 24 hours from the moment the financial entity has become aware of the incident, and an intermediate report, at the latest, within 72 hours. Likewise, VARA requires VASPs to report material cybersecurity events or events triggering the BCDR plan that materially impact business operations to VARA as soon as reasonably practicable, and in any event no later than 72 hours from detection. The cybersecurity policy that all VASPs are required to have in place must include provisions for incident response, highlighting the importance both regulators place on cybersecurity events as a growing source of concern in terms of operational and systemic risk.

IV. Smart Contract Auditability

31. While smart contract auditability is not mandatory under MiCAR, EU CASPs must include in the crypto-asset White Papers information on whether an audit of the underlying technology was conducted, and on the outcome of such audit.[22] In comparison, VARA requires VASPs to ensure that all smart contracts used for VAs have undergone comprehensive audits of their effectiveness,

---

21 According to the draft published under the Final Report on RTS and ITS on content, format, timelines, and procedures for reporting of major incidents and significant cyber threats under DORA.

22 Commission Implementing Regulation (EU) 2024/2984 of 29 November 2024 laying down implementing technical standards for the application of Regulation (EU) 2023/1114 of the European Parliament and of the Council with regard to forms, formats and templates for the crypto-asset white papers.

enforceability, and robustness, and that findings are remediated. Additionally, mandatory vulnerability assessments and penetration testing (as described above) should include comprehensive audits of smart contracts relevant to VASPs' business.

V. Critical Outsourcing Arrangements

32. MiCAR and VARA take distinct approaches to the regulation of critical outsourcing arrangements, reflecting their respective supervisory philosophies. MiCAR adopts a structured and harmonised framework aligned with existing EU financial regulation, requiring CASPs to ensure that critical outsourcing, particularly of custody, IT systems, and cloud infrastructure, does not impair regulatory compliance, service continuity, or supervisory oversight. CASPs must maintain detailed contractual agreements, conduct due diligence, and ensure that regulators retain effective access and audit rights over outsourced functions.

33. By contrast, VARA applies a principle-based, technology-focused approach, requiring VASPs to identify, assess, and manage risks associated with material outsourcing, particularly where functions involve core systems, wallet management, or third-party technology providers. The recently issued Technology and Information Guideline reinforces the requirement for accountability, transparency, and contingency planning, with a strong focus on operational resilience and local auditability. While MiCAR codifies outsourcing under a harmonised prudential framework, VARA's approach is more agile, enabling tailored controls that support complex Web3 business models without compromising regulatory visibility.

§ 8. MARKET CONDUCT

I. Financial Promotions

34. MiCAR stipulates a set of requirements for marketing communications relating to offers or admissions to trading of any CAs, which includes that all marketing communications be fair, clear, not misleading, and consistent with the corresponding CA White Paper. MiCAR also contemplates a separate set of obligations for marketing communications related to issuance or admission to trading of ARTs and EMTs, which includes the obligation for the inclusion of a disclaimer on the right of redemption against the issuer at any time and at par value, and a prohibition on dissemination before the publication of the CA White Paper.

35. Similar to MiCAR's approach, VARA requires all VASPs to comply with the dedicated VARA Marketing Regulation, which includes the obligation for all marketing communications to be fair, clear, and not misleading. The VARA Marketing Regulation contains specific obligations if FRVAs or ARVAs are involved. For FRVAs, marketing communications must clearly state the right to redeem at par, and that the FRVAs are not covered by protection schemes. For ARVAs, specific conditions and disclaimers apply if the term 'stablecoin' is used.

II. Market Manipulation and Market Offences

36. Both MiCAR and the VARA framework impose rules to prevent market abuse, and explicitly prohibit insider dealing, unlawful disclosure, and market manipulation. In addition, VARA has specific rules for VASPs providing broker-dealer services and exchange services, to establish policies and procedures for the prohibition, detection, prevention, and deterrence of such market offences and abusive practices. Moreover, VASPs providing exchange services are also required to have systems in place that allow them to conduct market surveillance, detect market abuse, and to report information on potential abuses to VARA.

§ 9. GOVERNANCE REQUIREMENTS

37. MiCAR and VARA establish governance requirements for CASPs/VASPs, including fit and proper criteria for key individuals, internal policies for compliance and risk management, and obligations for record-keeping and reporting. MiCAR sets out high-level governance expectations, requiring issuers of ARTs to implement robust arrangements with clear structures, risk controls, and internal procedures, while other CASPs are only required to describe their governance arrangements. Member States are responsible for detailing these requirements further. In contrast, VARA provides a more comprehensive and detailed framework in its Company Rulebook,[23] mandating a transparent company structure, segregation-of-duties and conflicts-of-interest policies, board oversight, and regular updates to governance documents.

Fit and Proper Requirements

38. MiCAR requires members of the management body and qualifying shareholders of ART issuers and CASPs to be fit and proper and of sufficiently good repute. VARA requires key officers (members of the board of directors, responsible individuals, and certain key function holders such as the Compliance Officer, Money Laundering Reporting Officer, and other individuals as determined by VARA) to meet these criteria. Under MiCAR, members of the management body (and other specific individuals defined at national level), as

[23] https://rulebooks.vara.ae/rulebook/company-rulebook.

well as shareholders that have qualifying participation, are subject to fit and proper assessments.

39. The frameworks under MiCAR and VARA have detailed criteria for assessing whether an individual is a fit and proper person, which are mostly aligned. This assessment considers qualifications and relevant experience, honesty, integrity, and good reputation, for the purpose of which previous criminal convictions for financial misconduct, fraud, AML/CFT breaches, and market offences are considered. VARA also looks at financial soundness, which is not a stand-alone criterion in the EU framework.

§ 10. SPECIFIC REQUIREMENTS FOR VA ISSUERS

40. A comparative assessment of the CA/VA issuance frameworks under MiCAR and VARA is essential, as it reveals fundamental differences in regulatory design, scope, and strategic intent. MiCAR provides a detailed and prescriptive framework specifically for the issuance of ARTs and EMTs, introducing issuer obligations akin to those in traditional financial markets, including White Paper disclosures, capital requirements, and prior approval by competent authorities. However, for the issuance of other CAs, such as utility tokens, MiCAR adopts a lighter approach, with no prior authorisation required and only basic transparency obligations. In contrast, VARA establishes a broader and more comprehensive regime for all forms of VA issuance, regardless of their economic function, including payment, investment, or utility characteristics. Through its bespoke ARVA and FRVA framework and overarching licensing framework, VARA mandates prior approval, governance assessments, and detailed disclosure requirements tailored to the nature and complexity of each issuance. Similarly, VARA introduced the Category 2 Issuance for VAs, which does not require an authorisation from VARA, based on the nature and purpose of such VAs. This difference underscores MiCAR's product-based, risk-tiered focus versus VARA's activity-based, all-encompassing model, highlighting the strategic divergence between regulatory harmonisation and innovation-oriented oversight.

I. Licensing Regime

41. MiCAR requires ART issuers to be authorised (unless exempt), and comply with governance, risk management, internal control, audit, own funds, reserve of assets, and custody rules. EMT issuers must be authorised credit institutions or electronic money institutions and comply with e-money rules regarding issuance and redemption, to be able to issue.

42. VARA classifies VA issuances 'in the course of a business' in two categories: Category 1 (requires VARA licence, includes FRVAs/ARVAs) and

Category 2 (no VARA licence required, but placement and distribution must be via a licensed distributor). For Category 1 issuance, issuers need to comply with the VARA Mandatory Rulebooks and specific FRVA and ARVA rules, depending on the asset they intend to issue. FRVA issuers must comply with rules on reserve assets (100% backing using specific institutions, segregation, assurance of timely access, monthly disclosure of reserve asset composition, and heightened independent audit requirements) and redemption at par. ARVA issuers (especially those purporting stable value) must demonstrate the basis for value, hold sufficient or acceptable reserve assets (managed prudently, segregated), undergo independent audits, and specify redemption rights or procedures if offered.

II. Significant Issuers

43. MiCAR requires authorisation for ART issuers, with exemptions for small offers or qualified investors. The authorisation process involves a detailed assessment by the competent authority, including consultation with ESAs and the European Central Bank ("**ECB**") or national central bank. EBA is mandated to directly supervise issuers of significant ARTs and EMTs, with limited exceptions. Issuers of ARTs and EMTs may be classified as such if they meet certain criteria related to size, usage, issuer influence, or financial system links. These include factors like size of user base, transaction volume, market value, or the issuer's broader crypto activities. EBA makes the decision on the classification after consulting the relevant competent authorities.

44. VARA requires VASPs to carry out a fully fledged licensing process for Category 1 VA issuance. VARA may at its sole discretion designate a VASP as a significant FRVA or ARVA Issuer based on numerous factors, such as the number of VA holders, transaction volume, reserve assets, and the VASP's activities or complexity. Once designated, VARA can impose additional regulatory requirements beyond standard rules, covering areas like governance, capital requirements, mandatory audits and reporting obligations.

III. Reserve Composition

45. Under MiCAR, issuers of ARTs are required to establish and maintain a fully segregated reserve of assets that covers the risks associated with the tokens and ensures liquidity for redemption rights. This reserve must be legally and operationally distinct from the issuer's own assets and those of other tokens, and its composition, management, and valuation must adhere to stringent liquidity and risk management standards, including mandatory audits every six months. The reserve assets must be held in custody by qualified, independent custodians and must not be encumbered or pledged. Investments of reserve assets are restricted to highly liquid and low-risk instruments, and all profits or losses from such investments are borne by the issuer. This framework is also applicable to issuers of significant EMTs.

46. Similarly, VARA requires FRVA issuers to hold reserve assets corresponding to at least 100% of the FRVAs in circulation, denominated in the referenced currency or currencies in highly liquid instruments, and held in specified highly secure institutions (CBUAE, licensed UAE banks, or licensed foreign bank branches in UAE). These must be legally segregated and structured to ensure prompt access for redemption and potential VARA intervention. ARVA issuers (if purporting stable value) must hold sufficient reserve assets, following specific rules for composition, prudent management, segregation, and guarantee that assets are unencumbered to secure risks and mitigate liquidity risks.

47. Both the VARA framework and MiCAR include periodic external audit requirements. For ART issuers and significant EMT issuers, independent audit of reserve assets is mandatory at least every six months. VARA also requires an independent audit of reserve assets for FRVAs, with a minimum periodicity of at least one month, and for ARVAs at least every six months.

IV. White Paper Disclosures

48. MiCAR requires a CA White Paper for offers and admissions to trading of CAs (unless exempt), including for ARTs and EMTs (with variations in approval and notification). The White Paper must be fair, clear, not misleading, and contain mandatory disclosures on issuance or offering and token details, underlying technology and functionalities, and risks. Specific content is required for ARTs (related to stabilisation mechanism, reserve assets, custodial arrangements, and rights) and EMTs (related to redemption rights).

49. VARA requires a White Paper and risk disclosure statement for most VA issuances 'in the course of a business' (excluding Exempt VAs). The White Paper must contain minimum disclosures specified by VARA, be machine-readable, and the issuer (for Category 1 VAs) or licensed distributor (for Category 2 VAs) is responsible for its accuracy and completeness. The White Paper content includes detailed information on the issuer, key personnel, used distributed ledger technology, VA features, environmental impact, and offer details. VARA includes additional White Paper disclosures for ARVA issuers to further describe reserve asset composition and reference asset[24] safeguards.

---

[24] VARA defines ARVAs by reference to Real World Assets (RWAs), other ARVAs, or a combination. VARA's ARVA rules address RWAs specifically, requiring clear descriptions of granted rights and value, how value is maintained, reference asset composition, direct ownership rights (if any), and how legal and regulatory requirements for settlement or transfer of underlying reference assets are met.

V. Rights and Obligations of Token-holders

50. MiCAR requires offerors and persons seeking admission to trading of CAs other than ARTs and EMTs to act in the best interests of holders and treat holders equally and fairly (unless otherwise disclosed in the White Paper). ART and EMT issuers must provide fair and clear information, abstain from any misleading information, and ensure ongoing disclosure. Token holders benefit from reserve assets in case of insolvency and must be protected by redemption rights.

51. VARA requires client agreements to state that ownership of client assets remains with the client, and FRVA and ARVA White Papers must describe the rights and obligations of the token holders in detail. Civil liability for misleading White Papers applies in both regimes.

52. MiCAR requires EMT issuers to ensure holders can redeem at any time, at par value, against the referenced currency. ART issuers must have a procedure for redemption, a recovery plan that can lead to suspension of redemption by the competent authority, and an orderly redemption plan for discontinuation. VARA requires FRVA issuers to ensure that VA holders have the legal right to redeem at par and that such requests are processed promptly. ARVA issuers, if offering redemption, must ensure that holders can redeem for equal value in UAE dirham or other forms, processed within a reasonable period and without fees. Redemption procedures must be detailed in the White Paper in both cases.

§ 11. SUPERVISION AND ENFORCEMENT

53. Under both MiCAR and the VARA framework, competent authorities share core supervisory and enforcement powers, including the power to conduct inspections and investigations, request information (e.g. data, documents, books, and records), take voluntary statements and testimony, issue orders and directives, and suspend, limit, or prohibit services and trading activities. Under MiCAR, national competent authorities shall be designated in each Member State, and supervisory responsibilities for significant asset-referenced and e-money tokens are transferred to the EBA, with limited exceptions. MiCAR also includes powers to freeze assets and to require amendments to White Papers and marketing materials. In contrast, VARA is the sole authority in Dubai, with broad discretionary powers, such as objecting to outsourcing arrangements and suspending margin trading.

54. In terms of sanctions and penalties, MiCAR requires competent authorities to have the powers to impose administrative penalties and enforcement measures on issuers and CASPs, including public statements disclosing infringements, cease-and-desist orders, and fines on CASPs, issuers, and individuals. Likewise,

VARA's enforcement actions may include written reprimands, enforcement notices, limiting or revoking licences, imposing fines on both VASPs and selected individuals within the organisational structure, or any other action VARA considers necessary.

55. While both frameworks share a commitment to robust oversight and market protection, MiCAR emphasises harmonisation across the EU and coordination among multiple authorities, whereas VARA centralises regulatory control within a single, agile body tailored to Dubai's evolving VA landscape.

CHAPTER 3
REGULATION OF PROFESSIONALS IN THE EMIRATES

André Abou Aad

SECTION I. WHAT IS THE CURRENT REGULATORY FRAMEWORK FOR DIGITAL ASSETS IN THE UNITED ARAB EMIRATES (UAE)?

§ 1. OVERVIEW OF THE 5 UAE REGULATORY JURISDICTIONS AND REGULATORS

1. The UAE has no fewer than five jurisdictions, each with its own framework for regulating digital assets (DAs) and virtual asset services providers (VASPs). These rules apply only within the geographic area governed by the relevant regulator. For regulatory purposes, the UAE can be divided into:

(1) Mainland UAE, also called 'Onshore UAE', which spans the whole country except the financial free zones; and
(2) the financial free zones (FFZs), which act like independent regulatory islands. There are two FFZs: the Dubai International Financial Centre (the DIFC), in the Emirate of Dubai, and the Abu Dhabi Global Market (the ADGM), in the Emirate of Abu Dhabi.
Within this broad regulatory split, we can identify five regulatory jurisdictions where the main regulators are:
(3) In Onshore UAE:
   A. the UAE Central Bank (the CBUAE), which regulates stablecoins and the use of DAs in payment services;
   B. the Securities and Commodities Authority (the SCA), which regulates VASPs that offer services like advisory, brokerage, custody, exchange, and trading in DAs or securities in DA form; and
   C. the Virtual Assets Regulatory Authority (the VARA), which regulates activities that are broadly similar to those regulated by the SCA, only in 'Onshore Dubai', i.e. the Emirate of Dubai outside of the DIFC. The

VARA is the most recent regulator, which exercises its regulatory powers under a delegation from the SCA.

(4) In the FFZs:
  A. the Dubai Financial Services Authority (DFSA) regulates DAs in the DIFC. Its rules are mainly influenced by UK regulations (the DFSA also carries out its benchmarking against others); and
  B. the Financial Services Regulatory Authority (FSRA) regulates DAs in the ADGM. Its rules are similar to the DFSA's, but with some notable differences. The FSRA, although a younger jurisdiction than the DFSA, has placed great emphasis on developing its DAs regulatory regime in recent years.

§ 2. THE MAIN DIFFERENCES BETWEEN THE UAE JURISDICTIONS

2. One of the main differences between the FFZs and Onshore UAE is that the FFZs are common law jurisdictions where UAE commercial and civil laws (including financial regulations) do not apply – hence the analogy of a country within a country, or regulatory islands. However, UAE federal criminal laws apply in the FFZs. In practice, this means that anti-money laundering (AML) legislation applies in the FFZs, in addition to any AML rules made by the relevant FFZ regulator.

3. The FFZ regulators align their rules with international standards such as those of the IOSCO,[1] and the FATF[2] for AML. They also often benchmark their rules against rules in force in the UK, Australia, Hong Kong, and Singapore (among others).

4. Finally, each FFZ has its own court systems and judges, as well as the relevant authorities that are essential for the functioning of the FFZ (for example, the Registrar of Companies in the DIFC is the equivalent of Companies House).

§ 3. FRAGMENTATION OF THE REGULATORY LANDSCAPE

5. Given the plethora of options, choosing where to set up a VASP in the UAE can be challenging. This, naturally, gives rise to regulatory arbitrage. VASPs usually make their choice based on:

(1) The type of clients: The FFZs, being initially established as 'wholesale' jurisdictions, are a natural choice for a VASP that aims to cater to

---

1 The International Organization of Securities Commissions.
2 The Financial Action Task Force.

multinational institutional clients, since these are concentrated in the FFZs. By contrast, most, if not all, the UAE retail clients are found in Onshore UAE. Therefore, a VASP proposing to cater mainly to retail clients would be best advised to consider one of the Onshore UAE jurisdictions.

(2) Client location: Setting up in Onshore UAE has the distinct advantage of allowing a VASP to market its services freely to clients in Onshore UAE, without having to rely on one of the very few exemptions. On the other hand, if a VASP will be providing its services on a strictly offshore basis (i.e. only to clients located outside the UAE), then the FFZs may be a more suitable choice.

(3) Preferred legal system and rules: VASPs from outside the region may prefer the common law system in the FFZs, while regional and locally owned VASPs tend to favour the more familiar civil law environment. Most VASPs prefer to be subject to the FFZ rules, given the clarity and legal certainty these offer. However, some VASPs elect to be subject to Onshore UAE rules, mainly for political reasons.

(4) Choice of courts: FFZ courts are perceived as being more specialised, given that they are staffed mainly by experienced judges who are subject-matter experts. This offers a higher degree of efficiency and legal certainty than the courts in Onshore UAE. Note that a growing number of VASPs in Onshore UAE are technically allowed to, and often elect to, submit to the jurisdiction of the FFZ courts. Nonetheless, there is a higher likelihood that Onshore UAE courts will claim jurisdiction and apply UAE laws if a VASP is established in Onshore UAE.

SECTION II. HOW TO GET A LICENCE AND WHAT ARE THE MAIN CHALLENGES?

§ 1. COMPARING THE FFZS AND ONSHORE UAE

6. All UAE jurisdictions follow the standard two-step licensing process for obtaining, first, an 'in-principle approval',[3] then the final licence, if the applicant meets all requirements to the regulator's satisfaction.

7. However, in practice, Onshore UAE regulators follow a more procedural and bureaucratic approach than their FFZ counterparts. This means longer lead times and more document-intensive submissions. On the other hand, FFZ regulators tend to have a more proactive and substantive approach that affords a higher degree of flexibility in dealing with applications. This is especially invaluable for VASPs, given the novel nature of their proposed business. This

[3] This initial approval may have a different name, depending on the regulator granting it.

approach avoids unnecessary delays and is seen as the more business-friendly option for setting up in the UAE.

8. It is common for an applicant to have to adapt their business model and processes to the relevant regulatory requirements. Doing so in the FFZs may require fewer compromises. This is not only because the FFZ regulators have brought in dedicated teams who are familiar with the subject matter, but also because the FFZ regulators have a well-established process for varying or waiving certain rules that may otherwise pose an insurmountable obstacle to a VASP's novel business model. While this may also be an option in Onshore UAE, the practice of interactively engaging with the regulator to tailor the regulatory regime is not so well established.

9. Notwithstanding the above, the one common challenge all the UAE VASPs face is the considerable delays in opening bank accounts. The banks in Onshore UAE have been somewhat slower to get on board, and have traditionally been reluctant to open client money accounts for VASPs (although some banks are now addressing this, and the FFZ regulators are offering any help they can). Currently, opening a bank account for VASPs is proving to be very time-consuming, and is frequently delaying the VASPs' time-to-market.

§ 2. TAILORED RULES IN THE FFZS

10. Applicants in FFZs can actively engage with regulators to adjust the rules that apply to them, since the licensing process is often a two-way street which regulators often regard as a learning opportunity for them. This, of course, is possible only if the proposed novel activities fit within the regulator's risk appetite and regulatory policy.

11. In practice, FFZ regulators can tweak their regime by granting an applicant's request for a waiver or the modification of the rules. The changes requested can vary from a simple tweak (e.g. waiving the requirement for an authorised person to be resident in the UAE, if justified by the VASP's proposed business) to making sweeping changes which amount to the de facto enactment of a new regulatory regime (e.g. the variation of capital and client assets rules to adapt to the activities of a stablecoin issuer), all while the regulator puts together its new regime inspired by the VASP's application.

SECTION III. HOW DO UAE REGULATORS SUPERVISE AND ENFORCE THE RULES?

§ 1. ACTIVE SUPERVISION IN THE FFZS

12. The FFZs' regulators actively monitor their perimeter and compliance with their rules through regular and surprise site visits, as well as periodic thematic reviews.

13. On the enforcement side, the FFZ regulators have strong enforcement powers. For example, the DFSA is not limited in the amount of the fines it can impose, and both FFZs regulators can directly act against both licensed and unlicensed actors (e.g. the regulators can ban persons, prohibit entities from carrying on certain activities, or take action against market abuse carried out elsewhere if it has a nexus with the FFZ).

§ 2. REACTIVE SUPERVISION AND ENFORCEMENT IN ONSHORE UAE

14. Onshore UAE regulators are generally perceived as being 'reactive', in that they would normally take action following a complaint from a client, whistle-blower, or, less commonly, another authority. At the time of writing this chapter, we are seeing a surge in regulatory actions by the Onshore UAE regulators, especially in relation to breaches of AML rules.

15. While Onshore UAE regulators can impose administrative sanctions ranging from a warning to a fine, and even licence withdrawal, they can take direct administrative action only against licensed firms. This means that Onshore UAE regulators would need to refer offending non-licensed persons/entities to the UAE public prosecutor.

SECTION IV. WHAT TRENDS ARE EMERGING?

§ 1. STABLECOINS

16. Stablecoins are one of the top recent trends that are gaining significant traction.

17. The FSRA and the CBUAE have both introduced bespoke stablecoin regulations over the past year. This brought about an increase in stablecoin activity which has led to the adoption of DAs that allow payments for everyday expenses, such as government fees or paying for fuel at the pump.

18. However, there are major differences between the two new regimes, notably: ADGM issuers may offer yield-bearing stablecoins while CBUAE-licensed issuers may not, and any UAE dirham-denominated stablecoins can be issued in the UAE only by CBUAE-licensed issuers.

§ 2. TOKENISATION OF REAL-WORLD ASSETS

19. The tokenisation of real-world assets (RWAs) is the other recent trend which promises to unlock a whole new world of possibilities for investors.

20. The Dubai Land Department recently announced a pilot programme for tokenising real estate without having recourse to special-purpose vehicles. This is expected to spur the tokenisation of real property, which, in turn, would democratise investment in Dubai real estate, an important sector of the local economy that has surged dramatically in the past few years. Investors will be able to buy fractional shares in real property (off-plan properties are excluded, at the time of writing this chapter). Such tokens are touted as being liquid (talks for offering the tokens on regulated exchanges are under way) and easily redeemable, and may potentially generate a yield if the property is rented. With the Dubai real estate sector being particularly attractive to local and foreign investors alike, this world first is expected to generate significant traction in the coming years.

§ 3. PAYMENTS

21. One major application for DAs that is garnering particular interest is the use of tokens to facilitate the transfer of funds. Several new market entrants have begun offering this service, which is expected to enable round-the-clock instant money transfers and to do so in a way that is safer than traditional money transfers. The introduction of regulated stablecoins is also helping drive this trend.

§ 4. ANTI-MONEY LAUNDERING

22. AML remains a top concern that is always the highest on regulators' risk matrix. The UAE regulators are constantly monitoring new money laundering typologies and adapting their regulatory regimes, especially when it comes to DAs, which are typically perceived as a higher-risk asset. We can expect to see more adjustments to the regulators' AML regimes (like we saw with the 'travel rule') as the market further matures, as well as more enforcement actions.

§ 5. CUSTODY

23. As the VASP sector matures and the market grows, there will be an increased demand for more and better custody solutions. In that respect, while some UAE regulators seemingly prefer on-chain custody, others have yet to adopt an official stance on this.

§ 6. STAKING

24. Finally, staking is officially regulated by the VARA and the DFSA, and is recognised in FSRA guidance. Staking is expected to gain traction as more investors look to their DAs for generating a passive income, especially as yield-bearing stablecoins become available in the FFZs.

CHAPTER 4

AML AND CRYPTO-ASSETS: THE EUROPEAN REGULATORY FRAMEWORK

Pauline PAILLER

1. As soon as Bitcoin appeared and Initial Coin Offerings (ICOs) were developed to enable the issuance of tokens, concerns were raised about the risk of money laundering and terrorist financing. Crypto-assets, also known as digital assets or virtual assets, combine several risk factors by virtue of their very structure. Their genesis, in the aftermath of the 2008 subprime economic and financial crisis, was based on the fundamental objective of disintermediation in favour of peer-to-peer models. The aim of these models is to eliminate the need for a trusted third party, whose trust has largely been eroded as a result of the crisis.

2. Blockchain technology has been specifically designed as an alternative to traditional systems, enabling transactions to be conducted directly between participants without the need for a professional intermediary. Crypto-assets, which are stored in an electronic wallet,[1] can be managed in two ways: either by a third-party service provider who safeguards the user's private cryptographic keys through a so-called hosted wallet, or directly by the owner using software installed on a personal computer or mobile device, referred to as a non-hosted or self-hosted wallet. The holder of such crypto-assets may then engage in transactions – selling, purchasing, exchanging them for fiat currency or other crypto-assets – via public or private blockchains. These operations can be executed almost instantaneously and without regard to national borders, as crypto-assets are inherently devoid of territorial attachment. Furthermore, such transactions are conducted with near total anonymity – or, more precisely, pseudonymity.

3. These various characteristics contribute to making crypto-assets particularly conducive for money laundering operations, thereby exposing

---

[1] This wallet is associated with a private cryptographic key, which only the owner holds, and a public cryptographic key, which is used to identify the owner when carrying out a transaction on the blockchain.

users to significant – and, at times, extreme – risks. Although crypto-assets are inherently traceable, from the moment they are recorded on a blockchain – which is based on a decentralised register certified by a cryptographic process that records the public elements of a transaction, including the address of the originator's crypto-asset portfolio and that of the beneficiary – this traceability can be easily undermined. Regulatory authorities' analyses reveal that operators can obscure this traceability by engaging in multiple asset conversions. This is typically done via platforms that exchange crypto-assets for official currencies or other crypto-assets, or through the acquisition of non-fungible tokens (NFTs). Additional laundering techniques include the use of 'mining', whereby illicit funds are invested in computational infrastructure to participate in mining operations, with the aim of earning crypto-assets as a form of compensation.

4. Furthermore, although crypto-assets are traceable in principle, the identity of the wallet holder is unknown to the system. This means that crypto-asset transactions are technically anonymous or, more precisely, pseudonymous, as users are identified by their address on the blockchain (and/or a pseudonym), not by their name. However, pseudonymity is not fully equivalent to anonymity, as the actions of each address are recorded on the blockchain and can, therefore, be traced on public blockchains. Nevertheless, anonymisation processes can be employed through crypto-asset 'mixing' or 'shuffling' services[2] on private blockchains, to ultimately prevent tracing and guarantee the anonymity of participants.[3] While these services may be used legitimately for ensuring user confidentiality, they may also be used for criminal purposes.[4]

---

2 See EUROPOL, Press release, 'Multi-million crypto-currency laundering service Bestmixer.io taken down', 22 May 2019: https://www.europol.europa.eu/media-press/newsroom/news/multi-million-euro-cryptocurrency-laundering-service-bestmixerio-taken-down.

3 IMF/FSB, *IMF/FSF Synthesis Paper: Policies for Crypto-assets*, 7 September 2023, spec. p. 14: https://www.fsb.org/uploads/R070923-1.pdf. In French law, for anti-money laundering purposes, a recent law has introduced a specific presumption in relation to crypto-assets that supplements the presumption of money laundering in Art. 324-1-1 of the Criminal Code (see, applying it, Cass. Crim., 15 Feb. 2023, No. 22-81326). See Art. 324-1-1 of the Criminal Code, as amended by Act no. 2025-532 of 13 June 2025, known as the Narcotrafic Act: 'For the purposes of Article 324-1, assets or income are presumed to be the direct or indirect proceeds of a crime or offence where the material, legal or financial conditions of the investment, concealment or conversion operation cannot have any other justification than to conceal the origin or the actual beneficiary of these assets or income. *This presumption applies to any transaction carried out, under the conditions set out in the first paragraph of this article, using a crypto-asset with an integrated anonymisation function or using any type of account or technique that enables crypto-asset transactions to be anonymised or obscured.*'

4 For a definition of blender services, see ADAN, 'Les mixeurs entre vices et vertus', 20 December 2020, https://www.adan.eu/en/publication/les-mixeurs-entre-vices-et-vertus/: 'Blenders (or mixers) ensure the anonymity of transactions carried out via pseudonymous crypto-assets – such as bitcoin and ether. In effect, blenders are used in an attempt to prevent the tracing carried out on the public register of these crypto-assets. The techniques used by mixers to guarantee user confidentiality are very eclectic. A significant proportion of mixers operate using advanced cryptographic techniques (such as zk-SNARK) and pools

5. In recognition of these risks, the Anti-Money Laundering and Countering the Financing of Terrorism (AML/CFT) Regulations constituted the first measures adopted by the European policymakers to address the emerging threats associated with the use of crypto-assets.[5] Under European Union (EU) law, Directive (EU) 2018/843 of 5 May 2018, known as the fifth Anti-Money Laundering Directive, initially focused not on all crypto-assets or digital assets, but specifically on virtual currencies or cryptocurrencies, such as Bitcoin or Ether, which are conceived as units of exchange, lacking status of legal tender, and not issued by a central bank.[6] At the time, the regulatory scope was limited to service providers engaged in the custody of virtual currencies on behalf of third parties, as well as those involved in the purchase or sale of virtual currencies against legal tender (so-called 'crypto-to-fiat' services). It was only subsequently that European lawmakers expanded the regulatory framework to include all digital assets beyond virtual currencies, aligning with international developments following the amendments made in 2019 to the Financial Action Task Force (FATF)'s Recommendation 15 on new technologies.[7]

6. This harmonised framework for regulating crypto-assets in the broadest sense is anchored in three key texts. The first two, adopted on 31 May 2023, are as follows: first, Regulation (EU) 2023/1114 on markets in crypto-assets, commonly referred to as the MiCA Regulation, which establishes a framework for crypto-assets and related transactions, and formally recognises the status of crypto-assets service providers (CASP);[8] second, Regulation (EU) 2023/1113 on information accompanying transfers of funds and certain crypto-assets,[9] known

in which several token holders deposit their funds. These funds are then mixed together before being sent back to each of the recipients. At the end of the mixing process, each user recovers the same number of crypto-assets as they had deposited ab initio at the time of input. The crypto-assets recovered at the output will come from an address different from the initial address of the holder, which makes it possible to conceal the history of crypto-asset transactions. Mixing fees are generally set at 1% to 5% of the mixed amount.'

5 Regulation (EU) 2023/1114 of 31 May 2023 on crypto-asset markets (MiCA Regulation): see recital (4).

6 Directive (EU) 2018/843, of the European Parliament and of the Council of 30 May 2018 amending Directive (EU) 2015/849 on the prevention of the use of the financial system for the purposes of money laundering or terrorist financing, recitals (8) and (9). See Directive (EU) 2015/849, as amended by Directive (EU) 2018/843, Art. 3(18), which defines virtual currencies as 'a digital representation of value that is not issued or guaranteed by a central bank or a public authority, is not necessarily attached to a legally established currency and does not possess a legal status of currency or money, but is accepted by natural or legal persons as a means of exchange and which can be transferred, stored and traded electronically'.

7 FATF, *Virtual Assets and Virtual Asset Service Providers* (2019): www.fatf-gafi.org/publications/fatfrecommendations/documents/guidance-rba-virtual-assets.html.

8 See *supra*, for a presentation, 'The MiCA Regulation Methodology: Strength and Limits'.

9 Regulation (EU) 2023/1113 of the European Parliament and of the Council of 31 May 2023 on information accompanying transfers of funds and certain crypto-assets: RDBF 2023, comm. 165, note T. Bonneau.

as the TFR Regulation,[10] which brings all crypto-assets[11] – not merely virtual currencies or cryptocurrencies – within the scope of the AML/CFT system. It imposes enhanced due diligence obligations on crypto-asset service providers. For the sake of consistency, both regulations are based on a unified concept of crypto-assets, thus marking a definitive shift away from the narrower concept of 'virtual currency' used in the Fifth Anti-Money Laundering Directive. It is worth noting that the definition of crypto-asset adopted by the European policymaker aligns with the notion of virtual asset set out in the FATF Recommendations.[12] A third piece of legislation further contributes to the emergence of a coherent framework: Regulation (EU) 2024/1624 of 31 May 2024 on the prevention of the use of the financial system for the purpose of money laundering or terrorist financing; commonly referred to as the AML Regulation.[13] This Regulation reinforces provisions aimed at combating anonymity, with specific implications for the regulation of crypto-assets.

7. The measures introduced under the MiCA, TFR, and AML Regulations give rise to two main observations. The first is of a general nature: the cornerstone of the AML/CFT framework as it pertains to crypto-assets is the involvement of a CASP, at least at one stage in the transfer chain. The second observation follows directly from the first and highlights the inherent limitations of this approach.

SECTION I. THE PIVOT OF REGULATION: THE CRYPTO-ASSET SERVICE PROVIDER

8. The key place accorded to the CASP in the fight against money laundering is easy to explain. The main money laundering risks are based on the structural anonymity – or pseudonymity – attached to the characteristics of the crypto-asset registered on the blockchain, as well as on the cross-border dimension of transfers involving crypto-assets. The solution proposed by the European

---

10 For Transfer of Funds Regulation, which replaces the former Regulation (EU) 2015/847 of 20 May 2015 on information accompanying transfers of funds.

11 MiCA Regulation, above n. 5, recital (16).

12 TFR Regulation, above n. 9, recital (10): 'The definition of crypto-assets in Regulation (EU) 2023/1114 of the European Parliament and of the Council corresponds to the definition of virtual assets set out in the revised FATF Recommendations, and the list of crypto-asset services and crypto-asset service providers covered in that Regulation also encompasses the virtual asset service providers identified as such by FATF and considered likely to raise money laundering and terrorist financing concerns. In order to ensure coherency of Union law in that area, this Regulation should use the same definitions of crypto-assets, crypto-asset services and crypto-asset service providers as those used in Regulation (EU) 2023/1114.'

13 Regulation (EU) 2024/1624 of the European Parliament and of the Council of 31 May 2024 on the prevention of the use of the financial system for the purposes of money laundering or terrorist financing.

legislation is to impose obligations on all third parties who intervene in the transfer chain in a professional capacity, as they are in the best position to detect abusive behaviour.

9. Paradoxically, while the initial development of crypto-assets was founded on the principle of disintermediation – on the explicit aim of eliminating intermediaries – the current reality tends increasingly towards reintermediation, marked by the emergence of, and reliance on, a new category of intermediaries. These new intermediaries form the CASP category, which is set out in the MiCA Regulation, and is largely inspired by the investment firm category of financial market law. As a result, CASPs are subject to anti-money laundering regulations, and, when crypto-assets are transferred, the TFR Regulation imposes obligations on them to collect and transmit information regarding both the originator and the beneficiary of each transfer. A crypto-asset transfer is defined as 'any transaction to move crypto-assets from a distributed ledger address, a crypto-asset account or another device enabling the storage of crypto-assets to one or another, executed by at least one CASP acting on behalf of an originator or a beneficiary of crypto-assets'.[14] Therefore, as soon as a CASP intervenes in the transfer chain – either as the originator's,[15] intermediary's,[16] or beneficiary's[17] service provider – the rule of anonymity (or pseudonymity) will be broken, since this service provider will be required to gather information relating to the parties to the transfer. This applies even in the case where the transfer is initiated by or carried out on a self-hosted address. If the information is missing or incomplete, it will be up to the service provider in question to determine whether to carry out the transfer – if necessary, by modifying the initial transmission[18] – or reject, return, or suspend it.[19]

10. In the same vein, the AML Regulation underscores the risks associated with the anonymity of crypto-assets and the increasing opacity of transactions. It introduces enhanced due diligence requirements for transactions involving self-hosted wallets[20] and prohibits CASPs from providing and keeping anonymous crypto-asset accounts, as well as accounts that enable anonymisation or further

14 TFR Regulation, above n. 9, Art. 3(10).

15 Ibid., Art. 14 *et seq.*

16 Ibid., Art. 3(16): 'the "intermediary crypto-asset service provider" means a crypto-asset service provider that is not the crypto-asset service provider of the originator or of the beneficiary and that receives and transmits a transfer of crypto-assets on behalf of the crypto-asset service provider of the originator or of the beneficiary, or of another intermediary crypto-asset service provider'.

17 Ibid., Art.16 *et seq.*

18 See EBA, *Guidance on information requirements for fund transfers and certain transfers of crypto-assets under Regulation* (EU) 2023/1113 (hereinafter 'Guidance on Travel Rules'), EBA/GL/2024/11, 4.4.

19 TFR Regulation, above n. 9, Arts. 17 and 21.

20 AML Regulation, above n. 13, Art. 40 (Measures to mitigate the risks associated with transactions carried out using a self-hosted address).

obfuscation of transactions. This includes the use of anonymity-enhanced coins,[21] which are defined as 'crypto-assets that have built-in features designed to make crypto-asset transfer information anonymous, either systematically or optionally'.[22]

SECTION II. THE LIMITS OF REGULATION BASED ON THE CRYPTO-ASSET SERVICE PROVIDER

11. While the regulatory focus on CASPs and intermediaries appears to be a pragmatic and effective approach, this strategy is not without its shortcomings and uncertainties. These limitations stem from several key factors: the scope and definition of what constitutes a crypto-asset (1); the potential involvement of third-country providers, who operate beyond the reach of European regulatory oversight (2); and the possibility of disintermediated transactions, where no intermediary is involved at all (3).

§ 1. SCOPE AND DEFINITION OF A CRYPTO-ASSET

12. The definition of a CASP is primarily established by reference to the concept of a crypto-asset. The regulatory framework is thus unified around the definition set out in the MiCA Regulation. This includes both a technical definition (a CA is recorded in a *blockchain* using a cryptographic process) and a non-exhaustive classification into three categories:[23] electronic money tokens

---

21 Ibid., recital (160) ('The anonymity of crypto-assets exposes them to risks of misuse for criminal purposes. Anonymous crypto-asset accounts, as well as other anonymising instruments, do not allow the traceability of crypto-asset transfers, and make it difficult to identify linked transactions that might raise suspicion or to apply an adequate level of customer due diligence. In order to ensure effective application of AML/CFT requirements to crypto-assets, it is necessary to prohibit the provision and the custody of anonymous crypto-asset accounts or accounts allowing for the anonymisation or the increased obfuscation of transactions by crypto-asset service providers, including through anonymity-enhancing coins. That prohibition does not apply to providers of hardware and software or providers of self-hosted wallets insofar as they do not possess access to or control over those crypto-asset wallets.'). See also Art. 79(1).

22 Ibid., Art. 2(1)(25).

23 MiCA Regulation, above n. 5, recital (18): 'This Regulation classifies crypto-assets into three types, which should be distinguished from each other and which should be subject to different requirements depending on the risks they entail. The classification is based on whether or not crypto-assets seek to stabilise their value by reference to other assets.'

or e-money tokens (EMT)[24]; asset-referenced tokens (ART),[25] which are backed by a basket of assets, commodities, etc – these two categories referred to as stablecoins -; and other crypto-assets, encompassing a wide variety of crypto-assets, including utility tokens.[26] Accordingly, the scope of the TFR and AML Regulations mirrors that of the MiCA Regulation, although subject to specific exclusions.[27]

13. However, certain assets that are registered on blockchain and which may pose a clear risk of money laundering are de facto excluded from the anti-money laundering regulations because they fall outside the regulatory perimeter defined by the MiCA Regulation. This is especially true for NFTs,[28] which are expressly excluded from the scope of the MiCA Regulation. In this regard, the AML Regulation defers to a future assessment by the European Commission concerning whether and how NFTs should be brought within the scope of supervision and regulatory oversight.[29]

§ 2. INVOLVEMENT OF THIRD-COUNTRY PROVIDERS

14. Another significant limitation lies in the cross-border nature of crypto-assets transactions. A third-country service provider, not authorised under EU law, may be involved at some point in the transfer chain. While such an unauthorised service provider is prohibited from actively soliciting customers domiciled in the EU, it may still be engaged through reverse 'solicitation', whereby the EU client voluntarily initiates contact. In this case, regulated CASPs are required to establish monitoring and control mechanisms for such transfers. They must also apply enhanced due diligence measures to assess the risks associated with third-country service providers. Relevant risk factors include the following: the service provider is located in a jurisdiction subject to restrictive measures, including targeted financial measures; the country is not compliant with FATF standards; the jurisdiction does not impose any licensing requirements on service providers.

15. The TFR Regulation includes a review clause, requiring the European Commission to submit a report by 1 July 2026, evaluating the risks arising

---

24 Ibid., Art. 3(1)(7): '"electronic money token": a type of crypto-asset that seeks to maintain a stable value by reference to the value of an official currency'.

25 Ibid., Art. 3(1)(6): '"asset-based token" means a type of crypto-asset which is not an e-money token and which aims to retain a stable value by reference to another value or right or a combination thereof, including one or more official currencies'.

26 Ibid., recital (18). *Adde*, Art. 3(1)(9): '"utility token" means a type of crypto-asset intended solely to provide access to a good or service provided by its issuer'.

27 TFR Regulation, above n. 9, recital (23) and Art. 2(3)(3). See EBA, Guidance on Travel Rules, above n. 18, 4.2.1.

28 TFR Regulation, above n. 9, recital (24).

29 AML Regulation, above n. 13, recital (15).

from transfers involving entities not established in the EU. In parallel, the AML Regulation calls for the implementation of a coherent procedure for identifying countries presenting a risk[30] and introduces enhanced vigilance measures regarding cross-border correspondent relationships.[31]

§ 3. ABSENCE OF INTERMEDIARIES: THE DEFI CHALLENGE

16. The final point concerns cases where the transfer of crypto-assets does not involve any intermediaries. In the absence of a CASP, such transfers are not regulated. The development of decentralised finance, or DeFi, based on peer-to-peer models and the use of smart contracts, is a crucial issue[32] that should be at the heart of discussions on the adoption of a potential MiCA 2 Regulation, which will probably require changes to anti-money laundering regulations.

---

30 Ibid., recitals (85) to (88).

31 Ibid., recital (80) ('Cross-border correspondent relationships with a third country's respondent institution are characterised by their on-going, repetitive nature. Moreover, not all cross-border correspondent banking services present the same level of money laundering and terrorist financing risks. Therefore, the intensity of the enhanced due diligence measures should be determined by application of the principles of the risk-based approach. However, the risk-based approach should not be applied when interacting with a third country's respondent institutions that have no physical presence where they are created, or with unregistered and unlicensed entities providing crypto-asset services. Given the high risk of money laundering and terrorist financing inherent in shell institutions, credit institutions and financial institutions should refrain from entertaining any correspondent relationship with such shell institutions, as well as with counterparts in third countries that allow their accounts to be used by shell institutions. To avoid misuse of the Union's financial system to provide unregulated services, crypto-assets service providers should also ensure that their accounts are not used by nested exchanges and should have in place policies and procedures to detect any such attempt.'); Art. 37.

32 O. Fliche, J. Uri, M. Vileyn, Pôle Fintech-Innovation, *'Finance "décentralisée" ou "désintermédiée"' (DeFi), quelle réponse réglementaire? – Summary of responses to the public consultation'*, September 2023; AMF, *'Finance décentralisée (DeFi), Protocoles d'échanges et gouvernance: vues d'ensemble, tendances observées et points de discussion réglementaires'*, July 2024: https://www.amf-france.org/sites/institutionnel/files/private/2024-07/2024_defi_synthese-papier-discussion-amf.pdf.

TITLE 4
APPLICABLE LAW

CHOICE OF LAW UNDER MICAR: APPLICABLE LAW AND COMPETENT COURT FOR CRYPTO-ASSETS, SERVICES AND OFFERS

Matthias LEHMANN*

SECTION I. INTRODUCTION

1. The Markets in Crypto-Assets Regulation (MiCAR)[1] is transforming the legal framework of the crypto industry. It is mainly a regulatory text. Only a few of its provisions directly concern private law, such as those on the right of withdrawal and the liability for defective white papers or loss of crypto-assets.[2] Some provisions may have an indirect private law effect, for example by requiring the insertion of specific terms into contracts, or by prohibiting certain contract terms.[3] But the bulk of MiCAR concerns regulation and supervision. MiCAR requires Member States to impose particular duties on crypto-asset issuers, offerors, and service providers, and to monitor compliance.

2. Due to its focus on public law, MiCAR lacks provisions for determining the applicable private law. Still, it does not ignore the problem's existence. In

---

* Professor, University of Vienna and Radboud University Nijmegen. I wish to thank Paul Eichmüller, Lukas Petschning, and Fabian Schinerl for helpful comments. I am grateful to Charlotte Rieger for the linguistic and stylistic review and to Julia Wachowicz for her help with the manuscript.

1 Regulation (EU) 2023/1114 of the European Parliament and of the Council of 31 May 2023 on markets in crypto-assets, [2023] OJ L 150/40. The Regulation is sometimes abbreviated to 'MiCA', even by EU authorities: see, e.g. ESMA, 'Final Report: Draft technical Standards specifying certain requirements of the Markets in Crypto Assets Regulation (MiCA) – first package', 25 March 2024. This is inaccurate, as it merely refers to a market (in crypto-assets) and does not underline that this is a legal text (a regulation). See also the parallel abbreviation 'MiFIR' for Markets in Financial Instruments Regulation.

2 On the right of withdrawal, see Art. 13 MiCAR. On the liability for information in the white paper, see Arts. 15, 26, and 52 MiCAR. On the liability for lost crypto-assets, see Arts. 37(10) and 75(8) MiCAR.

3 For the requirement to include certain terms in the contract, e.g. the provisions in relation to custody and the administration of crypto-assets on behalf of clients, see Art. 75(1), second sentence, (g), MiCAR. For the prohibition of a certain term, see the prohibition of granting interest for asset-referenced tokens and e-money tokens: Arts. 40 and 50 MiCAR.

various instances, it calls for a choice of law[4] or requires indicating the applicable law and the competent court.[5] The failure to choose such a law can amount to an infringement of the Regulation, and even lead to supervisory measures, including fines.[6]

3. This raises the question of how the applicable law and competent court are to be determined, including if and to what extent they can be chosen. Any company wanting to offer crypto-assets or related services will face this question. The answer falls into the realm of Private International Law (PIL), which, understood broadly, encompasses both conflict of laws and conflict of jurisdiction.[7] The goal of this chapter is to explore the conflict-of-laws and conflict-of-jurisdiction rules that apply to offers of crypto-assets, their content, and related services. In addition, it will also address the possibility to arbitrate crypto disputes. These questions will be studied from the perspective of courts in EU Member States, where disputes in the realm of MiCAR are most likely to arise, and which the European legislator is likely to have had in mind when drafting the Regulation.

4. This chapter serves as a practical guide to crypto-asset service providers and issuers on how to comply with MiCAR's regulatory requirements concerning the applicable law and the competent court. But its scope is somewhat broader than that of the Regulation because it also covers crypto-assets that qualify as financial instruments, such as investment tokens or tokenised shares or bonds, which are excluded from the Regulation's scope.[8] On the other hand, questions on the law applicable to proprietary rights in crypto-assets, which have already

---

4 Art. 34(5), subpara. 2, last sentence (calling for an 'unambiguous choice of applicable law' in relation to contractual arrangements for asset-referenced tokens); Art. 75(1), second sentence, (g), MiCAR (requiring a choice of law in contracts for custody and the administration of crypto-assets on behalf of clients); Art. 82(1)(e) MiCAR (requiring a choice of law in contracts for transfer services).

5 Annex I, Part E, Point 19 and Part G, Point 10 (regarding the offer of crypto-assets other than asset-referenced tokens and e-money tokens and the tokens themselves); Annex II, Part C, Point 15 and Part D, Point 17 (regarding the offer of asset-referenced tokens and the tokens themselves); Annex III, Part B, Point 4; Part D, Point 8 (regarding the offer of e-money tokens and the tokens themselves).

6 See Annex V, Point 32 in conjunction with Art. 130(1) and Art. 131(1)(a) MiCAR (sanctioning the failure to provide an 'unambiguous choice of applicable law' in relation to contractual arrangements for asset-referenced tokens).

7 For such a wide understanding, see, e.g. G. van Calster, *European Private International Law*, 2nd ed., Oxford, Hart, 2016, pp. 1–2 (mentioning, in addition, recognition and enforcement of judgments).

8 See Art. 2(4)(a) MiCAR; on the subject of delineation of crypto-assets that are also financial instruments from those that are not, see M. Lehmann and F. Schinerl, 'The Concept of Financial Instruments: Drawing the Borderline between MiFID and MiCAR' (2024) 4 *Capital Markets Law Journal* 330.

been studied widely,[9] will be left out, except to the extent that they are closely connected to contractual issues.

5. This chapter has three parts, aligned with the structure of MiCAR, but in reverse order. First, it will explore the applicable law and the competent court for crypto-asset service contracts. Second, the same questions will be studied for crypto-asset offerings. Third, a closer look will be taken at the content of crypto-assets; that is, the law governing their content and the competent court for disputes arising from them.

SECTION II. CRYPTO-ASSET SERVICES CONTRACTS

§ 1. APPLICABLE LAW

6. Identifying the applicable law is vital whenever a contract for the provision of crypto-asset services is concluded. MiCAR requires such identification specifically from those who provide crypto-asset custody and administration services on behalf of clients.[10] However, for reasons of legal certainty and foreseeability, a similar clause is recommended for all other crypto-asset service contracts.

I. B2B Contracts

7. One means to identify the governing law is choosing it. For contracts for the provision of crypto-asset custody and administration services, MiCAR requires that the agreement 'shall include ... the applicable law'.[11] In practice, this will not only be a description, but a choice of the applicable law.

8. In contracts between businesses (B2B), a free choice of law is possible.[12] Any national law can be selected. There is no restriction to a specific legal system or range of legal systems, such as the law of EU Member States – third-country legal systems can also be chosen. In practice, the crypto-asset service provider will propose a choice of law in its General Terms and Conditions (GTC), which

---

9 See, e.g. M. Ng, 'Choice of Law for Property Issues Regarding Bitcoin under English Law' (2019) 15 *Journal of Private International Law* 315; K. Takahashi, 'Law Applicable to Proprietary Issues of Crypto-Assets' (2022) 18 *Journal of Private International Law* 339; M. Lehmann, 'Who Owns Bitcoin? Private Law Facing the Blockchain' (2020) 21 *Minnesota Journal of Law, Science & Technology* 93.

10 Art. 75(1), second sentence, (g), MiCAR.

11 Ibid.

12 Art. 3(1), Rome I Regulation (Regulation (EC) No 593/2008 of 17 June 2008 on the law applicable to contractual obligations (Rome I), [2008] OJ L 177/6).

the customer will usually accept. Although the parties can, theoretically, negotiate the applicable law, this is, in practice, a rare occurrence.

9. Regulatory law does not explicitly limit the freedom to choose the applicable law in B2B relations. However, MiCAR imposes specific requirements that the applicable law must achieve. For custody and management contracts, it requires the client's assets to be legally segregated from the service provider's assets 'in accordance with applicable law' in order to exclude any recourse by the service provider's creditors against the assets.[13] MiCAR does not say how this 'applicable law' is to be determined. Under traditional PIL, this issue is considered as part of property law. Although a wide variety of solutions have been proposed for the law governing property rights in crypto-assets,[14] such issues are generally governed by the law of the state where the assets are located *(lex rei sitae)*. Yet crypto-assets do not have any location, since they are stored on a distributed ledger that is typically dispersed worldwide. But where the crypto-assets are held in custody, they could be said to be 'located' at the custodian's place, if this expression is understood figuratively. While this solution seems attractive, it would mean that the custodian would find itself in breach of MiCAR if it is based in a state whose legal system does not grant the customer a right in the asset maintained in custody. To avoid this result, one could interpret MiCAR as obliging states to protect property rights in crypto-assets. This would also be in line with international recommendations.[15] An alternative solution would be to allow the choice of a foreign law that provides such protection. Again, this has been proposed on the international level.[16] If the latter approach was followed, custodians could choose a law different from that of their country of establishment or the place of custody, to comply with the requirements of MiCAR. For example, a German custodian could submit all assets it maintains to Austrian law. At the moment, however, such a conflicts rule has not been adopted by Member States.

10. Where no law has been chosen in the B2B contract, the custodian or manager of crypto-assets is still obliged to 'include' a reference to the applicable law in the agreement, which now means to specify the objectively applicable law. This law is determined by the general rules of EU PIL, according to which the service contract is governed by the law at the service provider's place of central

---

13 Art. 75(7)(2), MiCAR.

14 See, e.g. C. Wendehorst, 'Proprietary Rights in Digital Assets and the Conflict of Laws' in A. Bonomi, M. Lehmann, and S. Lalani (eds.), *Blockchain and Private International Law*, Leiden Brill, 2023, 107–26.

15 See also Principle 3(1), UNIDROIT Principles on Digital Assets and Private Law (2023) (recommending that states 'can' recognise proprietary rights in crypto-assets – meaning that they actually 'should' recognise such rights).

16 Ibid., Principle 5(3) with Principle 13 (stating that the law expressly specified in the custody agreement law governs the rights of the client who has put its crypto-assets into custody, especially in the event of the custodian's insolvency).

administration or principal place of business.[17] In the event that the contract is concluded or performed by a branch, the law at the place of the branch will apply.[18]

II. B2C Contracts

11. With regard to consumer contracts, the choice of the applicable law is subject to significant limitations. Consumer contracts are those concluded by a natural person for a purpose regarded as being outside his trade or profession (the consumer) with another person acting in the exercise of their trade or profession (the professional).[19] Under the Rome I Regulation, the mandatory rules of the state of the consumer's habitual residence apply regardless of the law chosen in the consumer contract.[20] Such mandatory rules include, for instance, those on standard terms control, information duties, or the consumer's right to withdraw from the contract.

12. However, the protection granted by the mandatory rules of the state of the consumer's habitual residence applies only to the extent that the professional either exercises commercial or professional activities in that country or directs its activities to it.[21] Where the consumer actively solicits the professional party (so-called reverse solicitation),[22] they cannot rely on the law of their habitual residence. This is, for instance, the case where the consumer uses a virtual private network (VPN) client or travels with their computer to another country to overcome geo-blocking measures taken by the service provider to limit its customer base and avoid the duties under EU law.

13. In EU PIL, a choice of law in consumer contracts is not entirely excluded: non-mandatory rules of law can be freely chosen.[23] Still, choice-of-law clauses must be drafted in a transparent way. According to the Court of Justice of the EU (CJEU), they must explicitly draw the consumer's attention to the continued applicability of the mandatory rules of their habitual residence.[24] This can be done, for example, by using the following suggested drafting:

> This agreement is subject to the law of [state X]. However, you can rely on the mandatory rules of the law of your habitual residence.

---

17 Art. 4(1)(b), Art. 19(1)(1), Rome I Regulation.
18 Ibid., Art. 19(2).
19 Ibid., Art. 6(1).
20 Ibid., Art. 6(2).
21 Ibid., Art. 6(1) *in fine*.
22 See Art. 61, MiCAR.
23 A different rule applies, e.g. in Switzerland, where choice of law in consumer contracts is completely banned: see Art. 120, Swiss Private International Law Act.
24 Case C-191/15, *VKI v. Amazon*, ECLI:EU:C:2016:612, para. 71.

14. Where no choice of law is made, one must differentiate: if the professional party is active in or targets the customer's country, the law of this country governs the contract;[25] where this is not the case, the law of the service provider applies.[26] Particularly where EU consumers engage in reverse solicitation of third-country service providers, non-EU law applies to their contractual relations with these providers.

15. Particular choice-of-law issues are posed by Article 13 of MiCAR. The provision gives retail holders (that is, consumers)[27] a right to withdraw from the contract within 14 days, subject to an exception for listed tokens. A crucial question concerns the geographical scope of this right. Does it only apply to retail holders in the EU, or also to those living in third countries? This problem is thorny and has broader implications beyond MiCAR. It concerns the interrelation between regulatory rules and PIL rules.

16. Firstly, it is clear that MiCAR, including the right of withdrawal it confers, applies directly throughout the EU. Given that MiCAR has relevance for the European Economic Area (EEA), it also covers Iceland, Liechtenstein, and Norway. But does this mean that the right of withdrawal is also granted to consumers living *outside* the EEA? Article 2(1) MiCAR, which states that the Regulation applies to the provision of crypto-asset services 'in the Union' (to be read as 'in the EEA'), certainly suggests such a broad scope. Seemingly, it covers not only services offered to EEA residents but also those by providers based in the EEA to third-state residents. After all, any provider with its headquarters or principal place of business in the EEA is offering services 'in the EEA', in the sense that they originate from there. Such a broad scope would also align with MiCAR's goal to provide a clear legal framework for cross-border services.[28]

17. However, MiCAR's direct applicability in all EEA Member States does not mean that the courts of Member States would be bound to apply the right of withdrawal to every consumer. In civil and commercial matters, the application of any legal rule is preceded first by an identification of the governing law. In doing so, the general rules of EU PIL (for contractual obligations: the Rome I Regulation) must be followed. These rules identify the law applicable unless the EU legislator wanted to diverge from them and create a special conflict-of-laws rule.[29] On reflection, Article 2 MiCAR does not lay down such a special conflicts rule. The provision is geared towards the regulatory goals the Regulation

---

[25] Art. 6(1), Rome I Regulation.

[26] Ibid., Art. 6(3) with Art. 4(1)(b).

[27] See the definition of 'retail holder' in Art. 3(1)(37) MiCAR ('any natural person who is acting for purposes which are outside that person's trade, business, craft or profession'). This is identical to the definition of consumer under Art. 6(1) Rome I Regulation.

[28] See Recital 6, MiCAR.

[29] The application of such special conflicts rules in other acts of EU law is explicitly safeguarded in Art. 23 Rome I Regulation.

seeks to achieve, and its broad and multiple criteria do not lend themselves to a multilateral conflicts rule. Article 13 MiCAR on the right of withdrawal is not an overriding mandatory provision, which would apply independently of the otherwise governing law, either.[30] Overriding mandatory provisions need to serve a public interest, as the CJEU has recently made clear.[31] The right of withdrawal aims at the protection of a supposedly weaker party, the 'retail holder'. Article 13 MiCAR, thus, is a pure private law provision, with no tangible public purpose beyond the protection of the private interests of the retail holders. Therefore, it is not an overriding mandatory provision.

18. Hence, the general rules of the Rome I Regulation must be applied first whenever the right of withdrawal under Article 13 MiCAR is invoked before a court in the EU.[32] This right will exist when the law of an EU or EEA Member State has been chosen (Article 6(2), first sentence, Rome I Regulation). If the law of a third state has been selected, then Article 13 MiCAR applies only under the condition that the consumer has her habitual residence in an EEA Member State and the professional either (1) pursues activities in this state or (2) directs such activities to this state, and the contract falls within the scope of such activities (see Article 6(1) and (2), second sentence, Rome I Regulation). In the absence of a choice of law, the right of withdrawal applies if the same conditions have been met (Article 6(1), Rome I Regulation). As a result, consumers living outside the EEA will not benefit from this right when an EU Member State court is competent to decide on the dispute, unless the law of an EEA state has been chosen in the contract with the crypto-asset service provider.

§ 2. COMPETENT COURT

19. Giving some thought to the competent court for disputes over crypto-asset service contracts is important, even though MiCAR does not explicitly require its identification. One reason is the applicable law, which will in part depend on the competent court, given that the court will always follow its national PIL rules to determine which law applies. The jurisdiction rules, therefore, indirectly determine the applicable law as well.

---

30 For the definition and effect of overriding mandatory rules, see Art. 9 Rome I Regulation.

31 Case C-86/23, *E.N.I. and Y.K.I. v. HUK-COBURG-Allgemeine Versicherung AG*, ECLI:EU:C:2024:689, para. 44.

32 The other EEA states who are not EU members are not bound by the rules of EU PIL, including the Rome I Regulation.

I. B2B Contracts

20. In B2B transactions, the parties may choose an EU Member State court to decide the dispute between them under the Brussels Ibis Regulation.[33] In contracts with parties from Switzerland, Iceland, and Norway, the courts of these countries or any EU Member State can be chosen under the Lugano Convention.[34] Some states have bound themselves to respect choice-of-court agreements, in the Hague Convention – for instance, the United Kingdom, Singapore, Albania, and Ukraine.[35] Others voluntarily accept a choice of their courts or a foreign court.[36] Where the parties seek to confer jurisdiction on the courts of a third country, the permissibility of this choice will, in most countries, be assessed under the law of the chosen court.[37] The right to choose the competent court is not restricted in any way by the regulatory rules of MiCAR.

21. Choice-of-court clauses are, therefore, immensely useful in B2B contracts. Typically, they need to be in writing or in electronic form (e.g. email). Here is a drafting suggestion:

> The court of [insert name] shall have exclusive jurisdiction to decide on any dispute or claim that arises out of or in connection with this contract.

22. Failing an agreement on the competent court, the general rules on jurisdiction must be followed. If the defendant is domiciled in the EU, the Brussels Ibis Regulation applies.[38] The Regulation allows claims relating to service contracts to be brought either at the domicile of the defendant[39] or at the place of performance; that is, the place where the service is provided or will be provided under the contract.[40] Identical heads of jurisdiction exist for disputes with defendants from the three Lugano Convention countries (Iceland, Norway,

---

33 Art. 25, Brussels Ibis Regulation (Regulation (EU) no. 1215/2012 of 12 December 2012 on jurisdiction and the recognition and enforcement of judgments in civil and commercial matters (recast), [2012] OJ L 351/1).

34 Art. 23, Lugano Convention (Convention on jurisdiction and the recognition and enforcement of judgments in civil and commercial matters, made on 30 October 2007 in Lugano).

35 See Convention on Choice of Court Agreements, made on 30 June 2005 at The Hague.

36 Examples are the United States, Canada, or Singapore.

37 According to some authors, derogatory effects from the jurisdiction of Member State courts should be cumulatively assessed under Art. 25 Brussels Ibis Regulation; however, this view is irreconcilable with the provision's clear wording to the contrary. See F. Garcimartin Alférez, 'Prorogation of Jurisdiction' in A. Dickinson and E. Lein (eds.), *The Brussels I Regulation Recast*, Oxford, OUP, 2015, paras 9.13–9.15.

38 For corporate defendants, the domicile is at the place of the statutory seat, central administration, or principal place of business: see Art. 63, Brussels Ibis Regulation.

39 See ibid., Art. 4(1).

40 Ibid., Art. 7(1)(b), second indent.

and Switzerland).[41] National rules of jurisdiction, which govern disputes against third-country defendants, can be similar.[42] It should be noted in this context that third-country entities are subject to MiCAR where they offer their services to EEA residents.[43]

23. Determining the place where crypto-asset services are provided, or are to be provided, is problematic, given that they are exclusively rendered electronically. In this context, the terms of the contract need to be taken into account.[44] Where they indicate a specific place, the court there has jurisdiction, unless its designation is held to be artificial, and was only inserted to change the competent court and circumvent the rules on choice-of-court agreements.[45]

24. In the absence of any contractual stipulation, the place of performance must be determined objectively.[46] Given that there is no tangible physical performance, one possibility is to consider the place of business of the service provider in general as the place of performance. In the case of a claim of the customer against the latter, this would lead to the special head of jurisdiction for contractual claims coinciding with the general head of jurisdiction at the defendant's domicile, thus depriving Article 7(2)(b), second indent, Brussels Ibis Regulation of its relevance. Another possibility would be to assume that crypto-asset services are invariably provided at the customer's domicile. However, this would introduce a head of jurisdiction at the claimant's domicile *(forum actoris)*, which had already been generally shunned by the drafters of the Brussels Convention, the forerunner of the Brussels I Regulation.[47]

25. Hence, it is necessary to determine in each individual case where a particular crypto-asset service was provided, or is to be provided, where no agreement on the place of performance exists. To facilitate this task, crypto-asset services can be classified into different types. For custody and management contracts, one could refer to the place where the necessary activities are carried out, for example where the entries on the blockchain are made. In the case of the

---

41 Art. 5(1)(b), Lugano Convention.

42 See e.g. § 88(1) Austrian Judicature Act *(Jurisdiktionsnorm)*; § 29 German Code of Civil Procedure *(Zivilprozessordnung)*.

43 See on the scope of MiCAR, *supra* Section I.

44 See Art. 7(1)(b) Brussels Ibis Regulation *in fine* ('in the case of the provision of services, the place in a Member State where, *under the contract*, the services were provided or should have been provided') (emphasis added).

45 M. Lehmann, 'Special Jurisdiction' in A. Dickinson and E. Lein (eds), above n. 37, para. 4.56. Austrian PIL contains an additional restriction by requiring agreements on the place of performance to be laid down in writing – § 88(1) Austrian Judicature Act *(Jurisdiktionsnorm)*; for details, see P. Eichmüller, 'Austria' in T. Lutzi, E. Piovesani, and D. Zgrabljic Rotar (eds.), *Jurisdiction over Non-EU Defendants*, Oxford, Hart, 2023, pp. 39–40.

46 Again, Austrian law is special in this respect, as it does not allow the objective determination of the place of performance: see ibid.

47 M. Lehmann, above n. 45, para 4.26.

operation of a trading platform, one could consider the place where the platform is operated as the place of provision of services.[48] If the service provided is an 'exchange' contract as defined by MiCAR, such as an intermediated contract for the exchange of crypto-assets against fiat money, the place from which the service provider operates the computer on which the transaction is carried out could be considered the place of performance; in the case of portfolio management, it could be the place where the portfolio of crypto-assets is managed.

26. These examples show that the place of performance tends to be the place of business of the service provider. It must be underlined, though, that this is not generally the case. Instead, one must try to identify, in each case, where the services were or are to be rendered. Where several services are provided in different places, the court at the place of the main performance has jurisdiction under Article 7(1)(b), second indent, Brussels Ibis Regulation, as the CJEU has ruled outside of the crypto context.[49] The CJEU has also made it clear that this place must be ascertained, as far as possible, on the basis of the provisions of the service contract itself.[50] Where this is impossible, the national tribunal must determine where the service provider has, in fact, carried out most of the activities.[51] Only if this is impossible, as well, may the court consider the domicile of the service provider as the place of performance.[52] This underlines the importance of including either a choice-of-court agreement or a clause on the place of performance in the service contract.

II. B2C Contracts

27. With regard to contracts with consumers, the special rules of Articles 17 to 19 Brussels Ibis Regulation apply, provided the professional party either pursues commercial or professional activities in the Member State in which the consumer habitually resides or directs its activities to this Member State.[53] If this condition is met, the consumer may be sued only at the place of their habitual residence, but has the choice of suing the professional party at the latter's domicile or the consumer's own habitual residence.[54] As a result, the competent

[48] It is true that this criterion fails in the case of a fully decentralised exchange (DEX); yet such exchanges are excluded anyway from MiCAR's scope – see Recital 22, second sentence, MiCAR ('Where crypto-asset services are provided in a fully decentralised manner without any intermediary, they should not fall within the scope of this Regulation'.).

[49] Case C-19/09, *Wood Floor Solutions Andreas Domberger GmbH v. Silva Trade SA*, ECLI:EU:C:2010:137, para. 36.

[50] Ibid., para. 37.

[51] Ibid., para. 40.

[52] Ibid., para. 42.

[53] Art. 17(1)(c), Brussels Ibis Regulation. These conditions are synchronised with those on the determination of the law applicable to consumer contracts under Art. 6(1) Rome I Regulation: see *supra* Section I, § 1, II.

[54] See Art. 18, Brussels Ibis Regulation.

court for crypto-asset services depends largely on the habitual residence of the consumer. An agreement on the competent court that is entered into before the dispute would have no effect.[55] MiCAR does not require the service provider to indicate the competent court in the contract or anywhere else.[56]

§ 3. ARBITRATION

28. Instead of selecting a competent court, parties may choose to submit disputes arising out of contracts concerning crypto-asset services to arbitration. This option is not excluded by MiCAR. Though Annexes I–III refer only to the 'competent court', arbitration remains a possibility. The obligation to identify the 'competent court' serves to bring the attention of crypto-asset holders to their potential means of dispute resolution against the offeror, regardless of the manner in which it takes place.[57] One cannot infer from the omission of the term 'arbitral tribunal' an intention on the part of the European legislator to prohibit arbitration, which has traditionally remained outside the scope of EU law. Instead, one must accept that MiCAR is merely silent on arbitration. As a consequence, it remains permitted where the general requirements are met.

29. Arbitration is generally regarded as a permissible way to resolve disputes in the private sphere. No specific EU rules exist with regard to the question of whether a specific dispute can be resolved by arbitration – that is, whether it is 'arbitrable' – or which law applies to arbitrability.[58] Hence, these questions depend on the non-harmonised law of the Member States.

I. B2B Contracts

30. B2B disputes arising out of a service contract will be arbitrable under the laws of most legal systems.[59] Service providers wanting to insert an arbitration clause in their terms are well advised to verify arbitrability under all national laws of the states to which they direct their services, to ensure the effective enforcement of any subsequent arbitral awards.

---

55 Ibid., Art. 19.

56 This contrasts with the requirements for public offerings, where the competent court must be specified in the White Paper: see *infra* Section III, § 2.

57 See Recital 24, MiCAR.

58 The Brussels Ibis Regulation explicitly excludes arbitration from its scope: see Art. 1(2)(d).

59 This is referred to as 'objective arbitrability'. In most jurisdictions, pecuniary claims are generally arbitrable: see, e.g. § 1030(1) German Code of Civil Procedure *(Zivilprozessordnung)*; § 582(1) Austrian Code of Civil Procedure *(Zivilprozessordnung)*. For a proposed transnational principle of arbitrability of business disputes, see M. LEHMANN, 'A Plea for a Transnational Approach to Arbitrability in Arbitral Practice' (2004) 42 *Columbia Journal of Transnational Law* 753–75.

31. Here is a drafting suggestion for an arbitration agreement:

Any dispute or claim that arises out of or in connection with this contract shall be finally settled by arbitration under the [rules of an arbitral institution]. The seat of arbitration shall be [city and country].

II. B2C Contracts

32. The possibility of arbitrating B2C disputes relating to crypto-asset services is severely curtailed in most states by provisions restricting the ability of consumers to enter into arbitration agreements. For example, Austrian law completely prohibits the conclusion of B2C arbitration agreements before a dispute has arisen.[60] In Germany, section 101 of the Securities Act restricts the validity of arbitration clauses in agreements with parties other than merchants, public entities, and private companies over securities-related services.[61] The latter provision covers only crypto-assets that constitute financial instruments, and thus are outside of MiCAR.[62] Because of its exceptional character and doubts about its compatibility with international, European, and German constitutional law,[63] it should not be applied *per analogiam* to services involving other crypto-assets, such as cryptocurrencies, utility tokens, payment tokens, or stablecoins. In those cases, arbitration agreements with non-professional parties would be valid under German law, but only to the extent that special formal requirements are complied with: the arbitration agreement must be contained in a written record or electronic document, which must be personally signed by the consumer and must not contain agreements other than those relating to the arbitral proceedings.[64] It may be extremely difficult to meet these requirements in practice, especially in the context of standard contracting.

§ 4. SUMMARY

33. For crypto-asset service contracts, one must distinguish between B2B and B2C contracts. In B2B contracts, the parties enjoy wide autonomy in choosing the applicable law and the competent court. For B2C contracts, restrictions in favour of the consumer apply, which generally point to the law and the courts at the consumer's habitual residence.

---

60 § 617(1), Austrian Code of Civil Procedure *(Zivilprozessordnung)*.

61 § 101, German Act on the Securities Trade *(Wertpapierhandelsgesetz)*.

62 § 2(4), German Securities Act *(Wertpapierhandelsgesetz)*.

63 On these doubts, see, e.g. M. Lehmann, '§ 101' in C.H. Seibt, P. Buck-Heeb, and R. Harnos (eds.), *Beck-OK WpHG* Munich, CH Beck, 2025, paras 17–27.

64 § 1031(3), German Code of Civil Procedure *(Zivilprozessordnung)*.

SECTION III. OFFERS OF CRYPTO-ASSETS TO THE PUBLIC

34. In its Titles II–IV, MiCAR regulates offers of crypto-assets to the public. This must be distinguished from the provision of crypto-asset services, which are governed by Title V of MiCAR. The dividing line between offers of crypto-assets and services related to them is not entirely clear. The notion 'offer to the public' is defined by MiCAR as 'a communication in any form, and by any means, presenting sufficient information on the terms of the offer and the crypto-assets to be offered so as to enable prospective holders to decide whether to purchase those crypto-assets'.[65] The offer is thus a preliminary step to a purchase contract. Among the crypto-asset services, MiCAR lists the 'exchange of crypto-assets for funds'.[66] In classic civil law terminology, this amounts to a purchase or sales contract. Before entering into such a sales contract, a service provider typically will make an offer to the public. As a consequence, it must comply with both Titles II–IV on offers to the public and Title V on crypto-asset services.

35. With regard to an offer to the public, MiCAR draws a further distinction depending on the type of crypto-assets: Titles III and IV contain rules for the public offer of stablecoins (asset-referenced tokens and e-money tokens) and Title II concerns public offers of all other crypto-assets. Stablecoins can only be offered by their issuers, who, consequently, must also draw up the White Paper. In contrast, other crypto-assets can also be offered by third persons, who may also seek their admission to trading on a trading platform. The issuer of stablecoins and the offeror of other crypto-assets are obliged to publish a white paper.[67] For private (international) law purposes, these details generally do not matter. Both types of crypto-assets and their offering will, therefore, be treated together in the following section. Only sometimes will specific rules apply for one or the other.

§ 1. APPLICABLE LAW

36. Service providers, issuers, or other persons offering crypto-assets in the EEA must identify the law that applies to their offers to the public.[68] For private

---

65 Art. 3(1), Point 12, MiCAR.

66 Ibid., Art. 3(1), Point 16(c).

67 See, for asset-referenced tokens issued by credit institutions, Art. 17(1)(a) MiCAR; for those issued by other persons, see Art. 18(2)(k) MiCAR. For issuers of e-money tokens, see Art. 48(7) MiCAR. For offerors of other crypto-assets, see Art. 9(1) MiCAR.

68 Annex I, Part E, Point 19, MiCAR (regarding offers of crypto-assets other than asset-referenced tokens and e-money tokens to the public); Annex II Part C, Point 15 (regarding offers of asset-referenced tokens to the public); Annex III Part B, Point 4 (regarding offers of e-money tokens to the public).

law purposes, the offer to the public consists of terms and conditions governing the contract between the crypto-asset seller and buyer.[69] The offeror must disclose the national law that governs these contractual terms and conditions. Taken literally, this is impossible: the offer itself does not constitute a legal relationship but only an invitation to trade *(invitatio ad offerendum)*. What the provision actually requires is a disclosure of the national law governing the prospective sales contract to be concluded between the offeror and the buyer. As this is a matter of contractual obligations, the applicable private law rules must be determined according to the Rome I Regulation.

I. Choice of Law

37. In B2B relations, the law governing the offer can be freely chosen.[70]

38. The same freedom applies to offers of most crypto-assets in B2C relations. This may be surprising, since normally party autonomy is restricted here by virtue of Article 6(2) Rome I Regulation.[71] Yet Article 6(4)(d) Rome I Regulation explicitly excludes from the scope of these rules 'rights and obligations constituting the terms and conditions governing the … offer … of transferable securities'. True, crypto-assets – insofar as they are governed by MICAR – are not transferable securities.[72] However, Article 6(4)(d) Rome I Regulation must be applied to them *per analogiam*. This is because the uniformity of crypto-asset offers must be maintained as well, as is the case for financial instruments.[73] The conditions for such offers must be the same for every investor in order to avoid discrimination. Moreover, different terms could lead to an increase of costs and risk, resulting in insoluble conflicts, for example in the case of over-subscription.[74] Against this background, the rights and obligations cannot depend on the habitual residence of the investor and the mandatory rules in

---

69 The definition of 'offer to the public' for regulatory purposes is wider and includes any information concerning these terms and the crypto-assets themselves: Art. 3(1), Point 12, MiCAR ('communication to persons in any form, and by any means, presenting sufficient information on the terms of the offer and the crypto-assets to be offered so as to enable prospective holders to decide whether to purchase those crypto-assets'). Obviously, it is impossible to identify a law governing such information. Hence, the rules referring to the offer to the public in the Annexes of MiCAR (ibid) must be understood to refer to the terms of the offer.

70 Art. 3(1), Rome I Regulation.

71 See *supra*, Section I.

72 On the distinction between financial instruments and crypto-assets, see M. Lehmann and F. Schinerl, above n. 8.

73 See recital 28, Rome I Regulation, for the rationale of exempting offers of financial instruments from the consumer protection rules.

74 See F. Garcimartín Alférez, 'New Issues in the Rome I Regulation: The Special Provisions on Financial Market Contracts' in A. Bonomi and P. Volken (eds.), *Yearbook of Private International Law*, Munich, Sellier European Publishers, 2009, vol. X, pp. 245, 252–53.

force there. Hence, Article 6 Rome I Regulation generally does not cover crypto-asset offerings.

39. However, the exception from the consumer conflicts rules only applies 'in so far as these activities do not constitute provision of a financial service'.[75] Many times, the offering of crypto-assets under Title II, III, or IV of MiCAR will be accompanied by services falling under Title V of MiCAR, such as the provision of advice, transfer services, or custody and administration of crypto-assets on behalf of clients. To the extent that such services are rendered, the exception in Article 6(4)(d) Rome I Regulation does not apply. In these cases, the individual relation between the consumer and the service provider is more important than the unity of the offering, and there is thus no reason to depart from the consumer conflicts provisions. As a result, Articles 6(1) and (2) Rome I Regulation will be fully applicable.

40. A similar solution also must be followed with regard to those crypto-assets that are admitted to trading on a trading platform. Although MiCAR deals with the admission to trading under the same title as the public offer of crypto-assets,[76] PIL treats them differently. For financial instruments admitted to trading, a special exception from the consumer conflicts rules exists in Article 6(4)(e) and Article 4(1)(h) Rome I Regulation. The latter refers to 'a multilateral system which brings together or facilitates the bringing together of multiple third-party buying and selling interests in financial instruments ... in accordance with non-discretionary rules and governed by a single law'. This is a very complex way of describing stock exchanges and electronic platforms on which financial instruments are offered.[77] Within the EU, such multilateral systems are regulated markets of exchanges and (electronic) multilateral trading facilities (MTFs).[78] The purpose of Article 4(1)(h) Rome I Regulation is to ensure that a single law applies to all transactions on these trading venues.[79] The wording of the provision directly applies to crypto-assets that constitute financial instruments in the sense of MiFID.[80] Examples are tokenised shares, tokenised bonds, or

---

[75] See Art. 6(4)(d), Rome I Regulation *in fine*.

[76] See Title II, MiCAR. See also Annex I, Part E, MiCAR, concerning '[i]nformation about the offer to the public of crypto-assets or their admission to trading').

[77] See M. Lehmann, 'Financial Instruments' in F. Ferrari and S. Leible (eds.), *Rome I Regulation*, Sellier European Law Publishers, 2009, pp. 85, 88; U. Magnus, 'Article 4: Applicable law in the absence of choice' in U. Magnus and P. Mankowski (eds.), *European Commentaries on Private International Law – Rome I Regulation*, Sellier European Law Publishers, 2017, para. 148; F. Ferrari and J. Bischoff, 'Article 4 Applicable Law in the Absence of Choice' in F. Ferrari (ed.), *Concise Commentary on the Rome I Regulation*, Cambridge, Cambridge, CUP, 2020, p. 117.

[78] See Recital 18, Rome I Regulation.

[79] F. Garcímartin Alférez, above n. 74, pp. 245, 247; M. Lehmann, above n. 77, p. 89.

[80] See Annex I, Section C, MiFID II (Directive 2014/65/EU of the European Parliament and of the Council of 15 May 2014 on markets in financial instruments and amending Directive 2002/92/EC and Directive 2011/61/EU (recast), [2014] OJ L 173/349). The Rome

derivative contracts.[81] These are financial instruments; contracts concluded on regulated markets or MTFs related to them are, therefore, covered by the exemption from the consumer conflicts rules in Article 6(4)(e) and Article 4(1)(h) Rome I Regulation.

41. However, the wording of Article 4(1)(h) Rome I Regulation does not cover crypto exchanges and similar trading platforms on which crypto-assets are traded. It deals only with multilateral trading platforms for 'financial instruments'. Crypto-assets governed by MiCAR do not fall into this category. Yet the provision should be applied *per analogiam* to transactions performed on a crypto exchange concerning them. In this respect, the Rome I Regulation contains a gap, which is explained by the fact that blockchain technology was still nascent at the time when the Regulation was adopted in 2008, and there were not yet any platforms on which crypto-assets were traded. Yet the problem regulated in Article 4(1)(h) Rome I Regulation also exists with crypto-asset trading platforms: the orders entered into the order book on such a trading platform cannot be subject to different laws because, otherwise, trading would not be possible. Thus, it is necessary to apply the provision to contracts concluded on such trading platforms *per analogiam*.

42. However, the analogous application of Article 6(4)(e) in conjunction with Article 4(1)(h) Rome I Regulation is not always justified. Many so-called crypto exchanges combine functions of crypto platforms with crypto-asset services, such as transfer services, the provision of advice, or portfolio management. These services are akin to financial services, so the consumer conflicts rules of Articles 6(1) and (2) Rome I Regulation also apply to them.

43. For the sake of clarity, it must be underlined that the analogy to Article 6(4)(d) and (e) Rome I Regulation suggested here only holds for crypto-assets issued in large numbers and in identical quality, such as cryptocurrencies, utility tokens, payment tokens, or stablecoins. It would not, for example, include NFTs, which by definition are not fungible and tradeable unless they are part of a large series or collection. These crypto-assets are not covered by MiCAR.[82] It is also not necessary to submit their public offer or trading to the same governing law. Therefore, the consumer conflicts provisions of Article 6(1) and (2) Rome I Regulation can be applied in full. This means that a choice of law is possible but cannot deprive the consumer of the mandatory provisions of their habitual residence, provided that the offeror pursued or directed its business activities to that country.

I Regulation refers to the now outdated MiFID I, which contained an identical definition: see Art. 94, MiFID II.

81 On the characterisation of crypto-assets as financial instruments, see M. Lehmann and F. Schinerl, above n. 8, 340–45.

82 See Art. 2(3), MiCAR.

44. To the crypto-assets covered by MiCAR, Article 6(4)(d) and (e) Rome I Regulation apply by analogy insofar as the parties enjoy practically limitless freedom to choose the applicable law in B2B and B2C contracts. This allows the offeror to draft a single choice-of-law clause which binds both professional and non-professional parties. This clause must be included in the terms of the offer. Here is a drafting suggestion:

This offer and its terms are governed by the law of [country].

45. Including this clause in the white paper does not suffice, as this is merely an information document which does not create binding rights and duties of the purchasers. The choice is not restricted to EU Member State laws; third-state laws can be chosen as well. It bears underlining that the choice does not affect the regulatory rules in MiCAR concerning the offering and the admission to trading, such as the limitations on the qualifying persons, the duties regarding marketing communications, or the duty to publish a white paper.[83] These rules apply independently of the private law governing the offering.

II. Absence of a Choice of Law

46. Failing a choice of law, one must distinguish where and how the crypto-assets are offered.

47. Crypto-assets can be offered over the counter (OTC) by a crypto-asset service provider in exchange for fiat currency. Curiously, MiCAR labels this an 'exchange' contract.[84] From a PIL perspective, one could consider this contract a 'sale of goods'. However, Article 4(1)(a) Rome I Regulation is not applicable because, according to the prevailing interpretation, the provision is limited to the sale of *tangible* products.[85] One could categorise the contract instead as a service contract, in line with its characterisation under MiCAR, leading to the applicability of Article 4(1)(b) Rome I Regulation.[86] Under that provision, the applicable law is that at the service provider's principal place of business or the place of the branch office which is responsible for the conclusion or the execution of the contract.[87] To illustrate, where Bitcoins are offered in Europe through a branch office of a US company established in the Netherlands, the

---

83 Ibid., Art. 4(1)(a), 6–9.

84 See ibid., Art. 3(1)(19), which defines the 'exchange of crypto-assets for funds' as 'the conclusion of purchase or sale contracts concerning crypto-assets with clients for other crypto-assets by using proprietary capital'.

85 See, e.g. D. Martiny, 'Rom I-VO Art. 4' in F.J. Säcker et al. (eds.), *Münchener Kommentar zum Bürgerlichen Gesetzbuch*, 9th ed., Munich, CH Beck, 2025, vol. 13, para. 32 and the references cited there.

86 See *supra*, Section II, § 2, I.

87 See Art. 19(1)(1), (2), Rome I Regulation.

offering contract would be governed by Dutch law unless a different law has been chosen.

48. For crypto-assets admitted to trading on a trading platform, Article 4(1)(h) Rome I Regulation applies by analogy.[88] Accordingly, in the absence of a choice of law, such offerings are governed by the law of that trading venue. However, this does not apply to crypto-asset services rendered by the operator of the trading platform, which are governed by the law of the service provider's habitual residence or, if the conditions of Article 6(1) Rome I Regulation apply, of the consumer's habitual residence.

49. For non-fungible crypto-assets which are not covered by MiCAR, special rules apply. If no choice of law is made, their offer is governed by the law of the offeror's habitual residence. In consumer contracts, the law of the habitual residence of the consumer is applicable, provided that the offeror pursued or directed its business activities to that country.[89]

50. In summary, offerings of crypto-assets covered by MiCAR will generally be subject to the chosen law or, in the absence of a choice of law, to the law of the principal place of business or branch of the offeror. If they are fungible and tradeable, they are subject to the law of the trading platform unless another law has been chosen.

§ 2. COMPETENT COURT

51. The distinction between B2B and B2C offerings is relevant for the determination of the court competent to decide disputes arising from crypto-asset offerings. Such disputes might concern, for instance, the attribution of crypto-assets to certain investors, or price fixing.

I. B2B Offers

52. In public offers to businesses, it is possible to agree on the competent court for the resolution of any dispute.[90] A choice-of-court clause can be included in the terms and conditions of the offer or be concluded separately. Merely mentioning a court in the White Paper required by MiCAR does not suffice, as the white paper is not part of the contract but only serves information purposes.[91] The agreement must be made in writing or in electronic form.[92]

---

88 See *supra*, Section III, § 1, II.
89 Art. 6(1), Rome I Regulation.
90 See Art. 25, Brussels Ibis Regulation.
91 See *supra*, Section II, § 1, I.
92 Art. 25(1)(a), Brussels Ibis Regulation.

53. If the parties have not agreed on the competent court, claims concerning offerings of crypto-assets can always be brought at the offeror's statutory seat, place of central administration, or principal place of business, at the claimant's election.[93] Alternatively, the claimant can use the head of jurisdiction in Article 7(1)(b), second indent, Brussels Ibis Regulation. While case law on the characterisation of crypto-asset offerings is still lacking, it seems reasonable to consider them as 'service' contracts for the purposes of the Brussels Ibis Regulation, given that, according to prevailing opinion, the 'sale of goods' category does not cover intangible objects.[94]

54. Article 7(1)(b), second indent, Brussels Ibis Regulation grants jurisdiction to the courts at the place of performance. This place can be determined by a clause in the offer, unless its only purpose is to circumvent the provisions on choice-of-court agreements.[95] In the absence of such a clause, the place of performance must be determined objectively. This is extremely difficult for crypto-assets, as they are delivered through a transfer on the blockchain, not in the real world.

55. Several solutions are possible. First, one could consider the domicile of the offeror as the place of performance. However, this would make the optional head of jurisdiction in Article 7(1)(b), second indent, Brussels Ibis Regulation coincide with Article 4(1) Brussels Ibis Regulation and, therefore, redundant.[96]

56. Instead, one must determine the place of delivery for each specific case. Insofar as crypto-assets are offered via a trading platform – for example, a crypto exchange – the place of the trading platform could be considered the place of performance.

57. In all other cases – that is, where the crypto-assets are distributed by the issuer itself or by a service provider outside of a trading platform – one must refer to the place in which the crypto-assets have been marketed and made available for acquisition. This will usually occur in many different places. In the case of a main provision at a particular place, Article 7(1)(b), second indent, Brussels Ibis Regulation is to be understood as the place of the principal delivery, as the CJEU has already clarified for the delivery of movable tangible goods.[97] This leads to a concentration of jurisdiction and facilitates collective actions. Where there is no such principal delivery, jurisdiction will be divided between different courts. While this may be inconvenient for the offeror, the

---

[93] Art. 4(1) in conjunction with Art. 63(1), Brussels Ibis Regulation.

[94] P. Mankowski, 'Art. 7' in U. Magnus and P. Mankowski (eds.), *Brussels Ibis Regulation*, Munich, Sellier European Law Publishers, 2016, para. 100. See *supra* Section II, § 1, I.

[95] See *supra* Section II, § 2, I.

[96] See *supra* Section I.

[97] Case C-386/05, *Color Drack GmbH v. Lexx International Vertriebs GmbH*, ECLI:EU:C:2007:262, para. 30.

fragmentation of jurisdiction corresponds to the purpose of the provision as defined by the CJEU, which is the sound administration of justice.[98]

58. The offeror can avoid such fragmentation by inserting a choice-of-court clause into the terms of the offer or clarifying the place of performance.

II. B2C Offers

59. In the event that offers are made to consumers, the special jurisdiction rules of Articles 17 to 19 Brussels Ibis Regulation must be followed. The usual condition applies; that is, the professional must either exercise commercial or professional activities in the Member State of the consumer's habitual residence or direct such activities there.[99] If this condition is met, the consumer can only be sued at the place of their habitual residence and has the choice whether to bring actions against the professional counterpart there or at the latter's domicile, understood as the statutory seat, place of central administration, or principal place of business of the issuer.[100]

60. As a result of the operation of the consumer protection rules, jurisdiction for the same offer will be dispersed over various courts. This fragmentation cannot be overcome through a choice-of-court clause, since such a clause is invalid in B2C contracts unless it is concluded after the dispute arises.[101] The offeror, who needs to identify the competent court in the crypto-asset white paper,[102] thus faces a problem. In light of the fragmented consumer jurisdiction, it cannot refer to a specific place. Instead, it needs to resort to an abstract description of the competent court. A drafting suggestion would be the following:

> The investor who is a consumer has the option to bring claims either at his/her habitual residence or at [insert statutory seat, the place of central administration, and principal place of business of the issuer, if different].

61. Where the offer is made to both professional and non-professional parties, this clause can be supplemented with a single head of jurisdiction for claims brought by professional parties. For instance, the following clause could be added:

> The investor who acts in a professional capacity can sue and be sued exclusively at [insert court].

---

98 Recital 16, Brussels Ibis Regulation.

99 See *supra* Section II, § 2, II.

100 Art. 18 with Art 63(1), Brussels Ibis Regulation.

101 Ibid., Art. 19.

102 See *supra* Section III, § 2.

62. It must be emphasised again that this is a contractual clause, which must be distinguished from the information in the white paper. The white paper should use similar language for the sake of consistency and transparency.

§ 3. ARBITRATION

63. Arbitration is also an alternative for the solution of disputes over public offers of crypto-assets. The same considerations already made regarding services also apply here.[103]

§ 4. SUMMARY

64. The applicable law and the competent court must be determined differently for the offering of crypto-assets. The applicable law can be freely chosen by the offeror in B2B offerings. In B2C offerings, the applicable law can be freely chosen where the offered crypto-asset is sufficiently similar to transferable securities, which is the case for all crypto-assets covered by MiCAR.

65. The determination of the competent court is different. While the offeror can insert a choice-of-court clause in the terms of the offering, such a clause does not have any effect against consumers. The latter cannot be deprived of their right to choose between the courts at the domicile of the offeror or the place of their own domicile.

SECTION IV. THE CONTENT OF THE CRYPTO-ASSET

66. Offerors of crypto-assets and issuers of stablecoins (asset-referenced tokens or e-money tokens) have the regulatory duty to indicate the law applicable to such assets, and the competent court for disputes concerning them, in the white paper they have to file.[104] How are these two issues to be determined?

---

[103] See *supra* Section II, § 3.

[104] Annex I, Part G, Point 10, MiCAR (regarding crypto-assets other than asset-referenced tokens and e-money tokens); Annex II, Part D, Point 17, MiCAR (regarding asset-referenced tokens); Annex III Part D, Point 8, MiCAR (regarding e-money tokens).

§ 1. APPLICABLE LAW

I. Scope

67. MiCAR requires an indication of the 'applicable law to the crypto-assets' in the white paper.[105] This can be interpreted in two different ways.

68. One possible interpretation is that the expression 'applicable law to the crypto-assets' concerns the law governing the rights in the assets themselves: more specifically, the proprietary rights or similar rights of entitlement *in rem*. However, indicating such law in the white paper would be close to impossible, given that: (1) most EU Member States lack clear rules, both from a conflict-of-laws perspective and a substantive law perspective; and (2) the law governing proprietary issues may change during the life cycle of the crypto-asset. For instance, the UNIDROIT Principles on Digital Assets and Private Law propose to determine proprietary rights in crypto-assets held in custody under the law of the custodial relationship.[106] As different investors will – in almost all cases – entrust various custodians with their crypto-assets, questions of property law will not be subject to the same legal system. Consequently, it is impossible to predict and state the applicable law in a white paper.

69. Therefore, it is more reasonable to interpret the term 'applicable law' differently, as referring to the law governing the *content* of the crypto-asset. Some crypto-assets create obligations for the issuer and rights for the holder. This is, for instance, the case for utility tokens, which give their holder a right to future goods or services and contain a corresponding obligation of the issuer to deliver or render those goods or services.[107] A similar situation applies to stablecoins, whose issuers often voluntarily provide investors with certain rights, for example to redeem their coins against others. It makes sense to determine the law governing the investors' rights.

70. Other crypto-assets, however, do not embody any rights. Typical examples are cryptocurrencies, such as Bitcoin or Ether. Since they do not create or represent any rights, it is unnecessary to determine a law governing their content. To underline this specificity, it seems appropriate not to indicate an applicable law in the white paper but to write 'n/a' or leave this space blank.

---

105 Ibid.

106 UNIDROIT Principles, above n. 15, Principle 5(3). For the role the custodian may play in determining the applicable property law, see *supra* Section II, § 1, I.

107 See the regulatory definition in Art. 3(1)(9) MiCAR.

II. Choice of Law

71. In B2B contracts, the law applicable to rights and obligations created by crypto-assets can be freely chosen.[108] To effect a choice of law, the issuer must insert a choice-of-law clause in the terms of the crypto-assets, which are typically published on the internet. A clause in the white paper does not suffice.[109] The choice is not restricted to EU Member State laws; third-state laws can also be chosen. The choice of law does not touch upon the applicability of the regulatory rules foreseen in MiCAR, such as the right of redemption or the prohibition of interest.[110] These rules are of a public law nature and apply independently of the private law governing the crypto-assets.

72. In B2C contracts, an unrestricted choice is only possible where Article 6(4)(d) Rome I Regulation is applied *per analogiam*. In the context of offerings, it has already been explained that the application of various rules of mandatory consumer law is inappropriate, as it would lead to investor discrimination, unpredictability, and obstacles to tradeability.[111] This is even more the case with regard to the content of the crypto-asset itself. Crypto-assets only exist in the legal realm; they are 'legal products'. If their governing law were to depend on the consumer's habitual residence, the issuance would be broken up into different instruments with diverging rights and obligations. Even worse, the content would change again with every transfer to a consumer with a different habitual residence, as the law of their habitual residence (or at least the mandatory provisions) would now govern the rights and obligations represented by the crypto-asset. To avoid this, the rights and obligations contained in these crypto-assets must be governed by one and the same law. Consequently, the first part of Article 6(4)(d) Rome I Regulation ('rights and obligations which constitute a financial instrument') must be applied by analogy to the content of fungible crypto-assets. The exception for financial services[112] does not play a role insofar as the content of the instrument is concerned.

73. However, as with offerings, an analogous application is only justified where the situation is actually comparable to that of financial instruments, such

---

108 Even though tradeable crypto-assets and negotiable instruments are generally analogous within European PIL, the exception from the Rome I Regulation for 'obligations arising under ... negotiable instruments' in Art. 1(2)(d) has no consequences for the content of the crypto-asset, as discussed here. This provision relates only to specific issues for negotiable instruments arising directly from their tradeability. In particular, it concerns issues such as the exclusion of defences: see M. Weller, 'Article 1 Rome I' in G.-P. Calliess and M. Renner (eds.), *Rome Regulations*, 3rd ed., Alphen aan den Rijn, Wolters Kluwer, 2020, para. 32.

109 See *supra* Section II, § 1, I.

110 Art. 39 and Art. 40, MiCAR.

111 See *supra* Section III, § 1, II.

112 Art. 6(4)(d), Rome I Regulation *in fine*.

as utility tokens, payment tokens, or stablecoins.[113] Where the fungibility of a crypto-asset is of no concern, Article 6(4)(d) should also not be applied, for example, for NFTs that are not part of a large series or collection. A choice of law remains possible, but according to Article 6(2) Rome I Regulation, it does not deprive the investor of the mandatory rules of consumer protection in force at their habitual residence at the time the contract was entered into.

74. In short, it is possible to choose the law governing the rights and obligations arising out of crypto-assets that are covered by MiCAR. This is true even with regard to consumers.

III. Absence of a Choice

75. Where a choice is lacking, the fallback rule of Article 4(1)(a) or (b) Rome I Regulation applies, depending on whether the crypto-asset entitles its holder to goods or services. In both cases, the content of the crypto-asset is governed by the law at the issuer's habitual residence, principal place of business, or branch office.[114] The issuer may or may not be identical to the offeror, but it is always the issuer's law that is decisive, as the issuer is obligated to fulfil the characteristic obligation of providing goods or services.

76. The consumer conflicts rules are also inapplicable where no choice of law has been made, by virtue of the analogous application of Article 6(4)(d).[115] However, Article 6 Rome I Regulation must be applied for NFTs that are not part of a large series or collection. For such tokens, the governing law will be the law of the habitual residence of the consumer, if the professional has pursued or directed its business to that country. If this is the case at all, the exception for reverse solicitation is not applicable, as the CJEU has clarified that the activities of the professional in the consumer's home jurisdiction need not be causally linked to contract conclusion.[116] Therefore, the consumer conflicts rules are only excluded if the issuer pursues no business activities in the consumer's home jurisdiction and does not direct any activities there either. In such cases, the law of the issuer's habitual residence remains applicable.

---

113 Cryptocurrencies are not mentioned here because they do not create any rights and obligations. Lacking any 'content', the question of which law governs their content does not even arise.

114 See *supra* Section II, § 1, I on Art. 19 Rome I Regulation.

115 See *supra*, Section III, § 1,I.

116 Case C-218/12, *Emrek v. Sabranovic*, ECLI ECLI:EU:C:2013:666.

§ 2. COMPETENT COURT

77. Disputes may arise over the rights and obligations represented by crypto-assets, for example where the issuer refuses to perform an obligation contained in a utility token. The determination of the competent court for such disputes follows the same rules as for disputes concerning the offering. Consequentially, professional investors have a choice between the domicile of the issuer and the place of performance.[117] Issuers can insert a choice-of-court clause into the terms governing the crypto-asset, which also binds legal successors.[118] However, such a clause does not bind consumers, who have the option to sue the issuer either at its domicile or at their own domicile.[119]

§ 3. ARBITRATION

78. Instead of choosing a competent court, issuers may insert an arbitration agreement into the terms governing the asset. Such a clause will be binding on consumers where the relevant arbitration law(s) permit B2C arbitration.[120] Additionally, the dispute must be arbitrable. This is typically the case where the dispute concerns economic matters.[121]

§ 4. SUMMARY

79. The law applicable to the rights and obligations resulting from crypto-assets can be freely chosen. This is also true in relation to consumers. Where crypto-assets are comparable to financial instruments, an unrestricted choice of law is possible. Regarding the competent court, the validity of a choice is limited to professional parties. Consumers have the option to sue at the issuer's domicile or at their own.

---

117 See *supra*, Section III, § 1, I.

118 Case C-366/13, *Profit Investment SIM v. Ossi and others* (for a choice-of-court agreement contained in a bond). Generally, the CJEU considers a jurisdiction clause binding whenever a legal successor assumes all rights and obligations under the initial agreement: see Case C-519/19, *Ryanair DAC v. DelayFix*, ECLI:EU:C:2020:1023, para. 47. This is always the case for tradeable crypto-assets, as they cannot be separated from the rights they represent.

119 See *supra*, Section II, § 2, II.

120 See *supra*, Section II, § 3.

121 For a comparison, see M. Lehmann, above n. 59.

SECTION V. CONCLUSION

80. MiCAR requires identification of the law applicable to crypto-asset service contracts, offerings of crypto-assets, and their content, in the white paper or in a service contract. The expression 'law' in this context means rules of private law, to be distinguished from regulatory rules that MiCAR itself foresees. The identification of the applicable private law has to be made in accordance with the Rome I Regulation.

81. In principle, the Rome I Regulation allows parties to freely choose the applicable private law. This choice can be made in the service contract, in the terms of the offer, or in the terms determining the content of the crypto-assets. However, restrictions may apply with regard to consumer-investors. In their regard, a dividing line must be drawn between crypto-asset services, on the one hand, and public offers of crypto-assets and their content, on the other. For crypto-asset services, the mandatory rules at the consumer's habitual residence cannot be derogated from. For the crypto-assets themselves and their public offer, an exemption from the consumer conflicts rules applies, as a result of which the governing law can be freely chosen. This free choice is necessary to preserve the integrity of the offer, to maintain the fungibility of the crypto-assets, and to avoid investor discrimination.

82. MiCAR also requires identifying the competent court for certain contracts concerning crypto-asset services and the offer of such assets (but not with regard to the content). Professional parties are free to select the competent court. Consumers, in contrast, are not bound by forum selection clauses. They can always sue at their domicile or at the defendant's domicile. This also applies to disputes arising in relation to the crypto-asset. The result is fragmented jurisdiction, which is deemed necessary to preserve the procedural privileges of consumers as presumptively weaker parties.

83. For crypto-asset offerors and issuers, managing the applicable law and the competent court is relatively easy. They can insert choice-of-law and choice-of-court clauses in the terms of their offerings and products, which will bind professional parties as well as consumers. Suggested terms for these clauses have been proposed in this contribution. Crypto-asset service providers are in a different position: they always have to factor in consumer protection when they choose the applicable law and competent court. In many cases, a choice of law in a crypto-asset service contract will not affect the mandatory rules of the consumer's country of habitual residence.

TITLE 5
TAX REGIME

THE EUROPEAN TAX REGULATION OF CRYPTO-ASSETS

Pablo GUÉDON

1. The emergence of crypto-assets, digital innovations with economic value, and their integration into numerous sectors, inevitably entail multiple tax consequences. Nevertheless, tax sovereignty has never been transferred to the European Union and remains largely the prerogative of the Member States. This results in a heterogeneous landscape of tax regimes applicable to crypto-assets, rendering it impossible to provide a unified presentation of these regimes in a book devoted to the European dimension of their legal framework.

2. This uniquely state-owned competence is subject to two major exceptions at the Union level: firstly, value-added tax (VAT) and, secondly, administrative cooperation in tax matters.

3. VAT is a harmonised tax governed by Directive 2006/112/EC, known as the 'VAT Directive',[1] the interpretation of which falls within the jurisdiction of the Court of Justice of the European Union. Consequently, transactions involving crypto-assets may raise specific issues of tax liability, territoriality, or legal classification that require the application of European Union law.

4. Moreover, the European Union has developed mechanisms for tax cooperation, notably through the 'DAC' directives (Directives on Administrative Cooperation), which concern the exchange of information between tax authorities and the reporting obligations of economic actors, whether taxpayers or intermediaries. These instruments aim to combat tax evasion and enhance transparency. Given the pseudonymous nature of crypto-asset transactions, which poses a challenge to national tax administrations, the Union has naturally intervened in this field with Directive 'DAC8'.[2]

5. This contribution thus proposes to examine the two main areas in which the European Union exercises its tax power in relation to crypto-assets. First, it will analyse the regulation of substantive tax law, i.e. VAT (Section I). Second,

[1] Council Directive 2006/112/EC of 28 November 2006 on the common system of value added tax.

[2] Council Directive 2023/2226/EU of 17 October 2023 amending Directive 2011/16/EU on administrative cooperation in the field of taxation.

it will explore the mechanisms of tax cooperation between Member States and the reporting obligations imposed on crypto-assets service providers (Section II).

SECTION I. REGULATION IN MATTERS OF SUBSTANTIVE TAX LAW

6. As previously stated, in relation to substantive tax law, European regulation addresses only one specific tax that concerns crypto-assets: VAT. In its approach to this novel and digital form of wealth, the VAT regime has shown notable adaptability compared to direct taxation systems such as income tax. The advent of blockchain technology and its various applications has not required amendments to the European VAT legislation, but has necessitated interpretative clarifications.

7. The key judicial decision in this area, following several divergent opinions[3] issued by the VAT Committee,[4] is the *Hedqvist* judgment delivered by the Court of Justice of the European Union on 22 October 2015.[5] Its legal effect remains unchanged even a decade later.

8. In that case, the European Court was asked by the Swedish Supreme Administrative Court to clarify the VAT treatment of a business exchanging bitcoins for traditional currencies. In response, the Court held, in line with the Advocate General's opinion, that bitcoins are analogous to national currencies – solely for VAT purposes – as their sole function is to serve as a means of payment.[6] Pursuant to the principle of fiscal neutrality, they must therefore receive equivalent treatment. The sale of thus falls outside the scope of VAT,

---

3 Value Added Tax Committee (Article 398 of Directive 2006/112/EC) Working Paper no. 811, Question concerning the application of EU VAT Provisions, Origin: United Kingdom, References: Articles 2(1)(c) and 135(1)(d), (e) and (f), 23 October 2014; Value Added Tax Committee (Article 398 of Directive 2006/112/EC) Working Paper No. 854, Question concerning the application of EU VAT Provision, Origin: Commission, References: Articles 2(1)(c) and 135(1)(d), Subject: VAT treatment of Bitcoin, 30 April 2015.

4 The VAT Committee is an institution tasked with promoting the uniform application of the provisions of the VAT Directive. It consists of representatives from the Member States and the European Commission. It is purely advisory and issues non-binding guidelines on the interpretation and application of the Directive.

5 CJEU, Case C-264/1422, *Skatteverket v. David Hedqvist*, JurisData no. 2015-023733; *Dr. Fisc.* 2015, no. 45, act. 608; V. C. Acard, 'Fiscalité financière', *Dr. Fisc.* 2016, no. 3, study 73. – *Comm. com. électr.* 2015, no. 12, alert 92, O. De Mattos; *Europe* 2015, commentary 516, note A.-L. Mosbrucker; T. Guillebon, 'Quel régime fiscal pour les bitcoins?', *Dr. Fisc.* 2015, no. 38, comm. 514; R. Vabres, 'CJEU, 22 October 2015, *Skatteverket v. David Hedqvist*, Aff C-264/14', *IRSF*, 2016, no. 1, p. 170.

6 For a critique of the decision – which the present author does not share – see L. Scarcella, 'Taxing cryptocurrencies. The VAT treatment of Bitcoin as a case-study', doctoral thesis, University of Graz, 2020.

as it constitutes neither a supply of goods nor a provision of services, given that currencies do not fit within either of these core VAT categories. However, the exchange of traditional currencies for and vice versa, when remunerated via a commission, constitutes a taxable supply of services within the scope of VAT, though exempt from taxation.[7] These services are performed in exchange for a fee corresponding to the margin between the purchase and resale prices.

9. Unfortunately, the Court has not issued any further rulings on this issue since 2015, despite the considerable diversification of crypto-assets in the interim. This silence creates uncertainty as to the VAT treatment of certain types of crypto-assets. It is clear that the *Hedqvist* decision applies, by extension, to crypto-assets analogous to bitcoin (including so-called 'cryptocurrencies' and stablecoins), in light of the reasoning adopted by the Court.[8] Conversely, it is equally certain that this precedent cannot be extended to other categories of crypto-assets, such as NFTs (non-fungible tokens) or those possessing the characteristics of financial instruments.

10. Only NFTs have received limited clarification from the VAT Committee, which has acknowledged their potentially diverse legal nature.[9] In short, the Committee has suggested that NFTs may constitute a property title (e.g. proof of ownership) if they grant rights over a tangible good, or that they may be classified as single-purpose vouchers (SPV) or multi-purpose vouchers (MPV) where they entitle the holder to receive goods or services. Furthermore, NFTs may also qualify as financial securities if they confer voting rights or a share in profits.[10] This European position is both welcome and insightful in relation to these specific assets and their potential diversity. However, it remains non-binding.

11. In the absence of EU-level normative intervention, national tax authorities have undertaken their own clarification of VAT rules as applied to the crypto-asset ecosystem. For instance, the French tax administration has outlined the VAT treatment of tokens issued through initial coin offerings (ICOs). The interpretative method used aligns with the functional approach adopted by the Court in *Hedqvist*. For example, the French tax administration has stated that, 'if the token confers upon its holder only the right to receive dividends and participate in the decision-making of the issuing company, it performs the same

---

[7] VAT Directive, Art. 135(1)(e).

[8] They serve no purpose other than to act as a means of payment.

[9] Value Added Tax Committee (Article 398 of Directive 2006/112/EC) Working Paper no. 1060, Question concerning the application of EU VAT Provisions, Origin: Commission, References: Articles 2, 9, 47 and 58, subject: Initial VAT reflections on non-fungible tokens, 21 February 2023.

[10] G. Person and T. Le Boucher, 'Régime TVA des NFTs: quels enseignements tirer de la dernière publication du Comité TVA? État des lieux de la réglementation TVA applicable en matière d'émission et de vente de NFTs', *Dr. Fisc.*, 2023, no. 25, Studies 220.

function as a share or equity interest and will be governed by company law rules'.[11] Otherwise, to establish the VAT treatment of tokens which do not meet the characteristics of financial instruments, the tax administration distinguishes two situations: on the one hand, tokens that allow someone to 'potentially' benefit from the provision of services or delivery of goods; and, on the other hand, those that give 'access to a set of goods or services determined at the time of the issue of the tokens'. In the first case, the existence of a risk on the very principle of future counterparts results in the absence of a direct link, within the meaning of VAT, at the time of issue of the tokens. Therefore, the 'sums received by the company issuing the tokens should not be subject to VAT'. The tax is due at the time these tokens are used by their holders to obtain an individualised good or service that could ultimately be produced by the issuer. In the second case, if the goods or services are determined at the time of issue of the tokens, the rules regarding vouchers are likely to apply.

12. However, this national approach carries the risk of divergent interpretations within the internal market. A striking example lies in the VAT treatment of mining activities. Countries such as Germany, France, Hungary, and Finland consider mining to be outside the scope of VAT due to the absence of a direct legal relationship between the miner and the parties to the validated transaction. In contrast, Austria, the Netherlands, and Portugal include mining within the scope of VAT, albeit as an exempt activity.[12] Such discrepancies in the interpretation of the VAT Directive for identical factual scenarios are problematic and call for harmonisation through a ruling by the Court of Justice.

13. Despite these various national and European positions, an overall trend has emerged: crypto-assets are generally assimilated into legal categories from the banking and financial sectors, which are typically exempt from VAT or fall outside its scope. This logic is mirrored by the United Arab Emirates Federal Tax Authority, which classifies most crypto-asset activities as financial services exempt from VAT.[13]

14. Beyond the VAT issue, European law has also intervened at the procedural and enforcement level to enhance the effectiveness of substantive tax rules, which remain primarily national.

---

11 BOI-RES-TVA-000054, 9 March 2021 (own translation).

12 N. Habibou and A. Vivaldi, 'La TVA face aux enjeux des actifs numériques: comment s'y préparer et quelles évolutions attendues?', *Dr. Fisc.*, 2024, no. 50, Studies 392.

13 Federal Tax Authority, Cabinet Decision No. 100 of 2024, 4 October 2024.

SECTION II. REGULATION IN MATTERS OF PROCEDURAL TAX LAW

15. The European intervention on oversight matters has materialised through Directive DAC8,[14] which addresses the fiscal monitoring of transactions involving crypto-assets. This initiative fits within a fertile international and European legal environment.[15] It is expressly linked to the well-known MiCA Regulation,[16] which entered into force on 29 June 2023. This European regulation sets out the main legal category used to define the scope of application of DAC8.[17] It is also inspired by the OECD's Crypto-Asset Reporting Framework,[18] a new component of the Common Reporting Standard for the automatic exchange of tax information. These international and European frameworks are developing in tandem, both in terms of timing and substance. On one side, the DAC8 recitals explicitly encourage Member States 'to use'[19] the OECD commentaries for the purpose of illustration or interpretation of the Directive's provisions, ensuring their coherent application across the EU. On the other, the OECD framework is in the process of becoming binding law: on 10 November 2023, the Secretary-General of the OECD announced that 48 states had agreed to implement the new regulatory framework by 2027. However, major global economies, such as China, Russia, Turkey are notably absent. Nevertheless, and of particular significance for this book, it should be emphasised that the United Arab Emirates, initially absent from the agreement, ultimately acceded to it on 21 July 2025.

16. Substantively, the Directive acknowledges that, while all Member States have enacted domestic rules to tax[20] these new forms of wealth, 'the decentralised nature of crypto-assets makes it difficult for Member States' tax administrations to ensure tax compliance'.[21]

---

14 Member States must transpose it no later than 31 December 2025, for initial application from 1 January 2026.

15 This contribution will only cover this aspect. The Directive also addresses the exchange of information on cross-border advance tax rulings and draws consequences from the judgment delivered by the Court of Justice of the European Union on 8 December 2022 regarding the articulation between the declaration of cross-border arrangements and lawyer–client privilege.

16 Regulation (EU) No. 2023/1114 on markets in crypto-assets, and amending Regulations (EU) No. 1093/2010 and (EU) No. 1095/2010 and Directives 2013/36/EU and (EU) 2019/1937, 31 May 2023.

17 'Regulation (EU) 2023/1114 defines the terms used for the purposes of this directive': recital 7.

18 OECD, *International Standards for the Automatic Exchange of Information in Tax Matters: Crypto-Asset Reporting Framework and 2023 Update to the Common Reporting Standard*, Paris, OECD Publishing, 2023.

19 Recital 9.

20 Although different from one Member State to another.

21 Recital 6.

17. To address this challenge, the Directive relies on intermediaries in the crypto-asset sector, who are deemed to be 'best placed to collect and verify the necessary information on their users'.[22] To that end, DAC8 Article 1(6) inserts Article 8(a)(d) and an annex into Directive 2011/16/EU on administrative cooperation in the field of taxation. These provisions impose reporting obligations on crypto-asset intermediaries, with the reported information being exchanged between national tax administrations.

18. The scope of the reporting obligation is both personal and material, involving several defined categories. On the material side, 'Reportable Crypto-Assets' are defined as any digital representation of value or rights that can be transferred and stored electronically using distributed ledger technology or similar, excluding central bank digital currencies, electronic money, or any crypto-asset that the reporting intermediary justifiably believes is not usable for payment or investment purposes. The Directive also clarifies that this category includes all decentralised crypto-assets, including stablecoins, e-money tokens under MiCA, and certain NFTs.

19. On the personal side, the reporting obligation applies to Crypto-Asset Service Providers (CASPs) regulated under MiCA, as well as to unregulated 'Crypto-Asset Operators'. In other words, for the purposes of the Directive, any actor offering 'Crypto-Asset Services'[23] qualifies as a 'Reporting Crypto-Asset Service Provider' when engaging in 'Reportable Transactions', which include all crypto-to-crypto or crypto-to-fiat exchanges, as well as transfers of crypto-assets to other addresses.[24] These rules apply regardless of whether the parties are individuals or legal entities.[25]

20. When these conditions are met, providers must report certain pieces of information annually, concerning users and their transactions. The data must be submitted, either during the calendar year following the relevant transactions or within the same year, to the competent authority of the Member State, where the provider is authorised under MiCA or is registered for the purposes of this Directive, in the case of unregulated operators.

---

22 Recital 12.

23 This definition refers to Art. 3 of the MiCA Regulation, which covers the following activities: the custody and administration of crypto-assets on behalf of clients; operation of a crypto-asset trading platform; exchange of crypto-assets for funds; exchange of crypto-assets for other crypto-assets; execution of orders for crypto-assets on behalf of clients; placement of crypto-assets; reception and transmission of orders for crypto-assets on behalf of clients; provision of advice on crypto-assets; portfolio management services for crypto-assets; provision of transfer services for crypto-assets on behalf of clients.

24 This other address may belong to the same taxpayer, or may be used for the payment of a tangible good or service.

25 Significant exceptions are, however, provided: notably, for public organisations, financial institutions, listed companies, and the crypto-asset service providers themselves.

21. The content of the information to be reported relates to the taxpayer users, the reported entity, and the transactions carried out. Regarding users, the information to be transmitted is, in summary, the following: name; address; Member State(s) of residence; a tax identification number; date and place of birth, if the user is a natural person; and, in the case of a legal entity, additional information on the natural person exercising ultimate control of that entity. The declared entity must also provide its name, address, tax identification number, and its legal entity identifier.

22. All of this reported data is intended for automatic exchange between Member States.

23. The establishment of this harmonised legal framework within the Union is a positive development for tax compliance. However, these measures have limited relevance for users and operations that take advantage of the full potential of the underlying blockchain technology, namely those that operate without intermediaries.

www.ingramcontent.com/pod-product-compliance
Ingram Content Group UK Ltd.
Pitfield, Milton Keynes, MK11 3LW, UK
UKHW051905290926
8980IPUK00017B/1779